School Choice

HERBERT J. WALBERG

School
Choice
the findings

CATO
INSTITUTE
WASHINGTON, D.C.

Library of Congress Cataloging-in-Publication Data

Walberg, Herbert J., 1937–
    School choice : the findings / Herbert J. Walberg.
        p. cm.
    Includes bibliographical references and index.
    ISBN 978-1-933995-05-2 (hardback : alk. paper) —
    ISBN 978-1-933995-04-5 (pbk. : alk. paper)
        1. School choice—United States—Evaluation. 2. Academic
    achievement—United States—Evaluation. I. Title.

    LB1027.9.W34 2007
    379.1'110973—dc22

                                                        2007025454

Cover design by Jon Meyers.

Printed in the United States of America.

CATO INSTITUTE
1000 Massachusetts Ave., N.W.
Washington, D.C. 20001
www.cato.org

Contents

Acknowledgments

I am fortunate to have been stimulated and supported by colleagues and organizations starting in graduate school at the University of Chicago, where I completed doctoral studies in 1964. The university supported interdisciplinary study, emphasized quantitative analysis, and encouraged doubt about conventional views—all of which were useful in completing the present book.

My present academic appointment at Stanford University's Hoover Institution enabled me, as a member of the Koret Task Force on K–12 Education, to meet twice a year and collaborate with its distinguished members—John Chubb, Williamson Evers, Chester Finn, Eric Hanushek, Paul Hill, E. D. Hirsch, Caroline Hoxby, Terry Moe, Paul Peterson, and Diane Ravitch. The members of this group hardly agree on all points about choice and other matters, but we probably would agree that our group discussions are among the most stimulating of our careers. They have led to the founding of the journal *Education Next*, the publication of a number of books, and evaluations of school policy in Florida, Texas, and Arkansas. I also acknowledge and thank Hoover director John Raisian, who sponsored work on one of my previous books on choice, *Education and Capitalism*, coauthored with Joseph Bast and published by Hoover Institution Press.

The National Center on School Choice at Vanderbilt University, sponsored by the U.S. Department of Education, has stimulated my thinking and writing about choice. My work there, including that on the *Handbook of Research on School Choice* and *Charter School Outcomes*, both coedited with the center's director Mark Berends and associates Dale Ballou and Matthew Springer as the beginning of a new series of books on school choice, has informed and motivated me in writing the present book.

I am honored to be a trustee, and to be stimulated by the other trustees, of the Foundation for Teaching Economics, which provides scholarships for high school teachers and students to study economics. Until his death, the foundation was advised by Milton Friedman, perhaps the most important school choice leader of modern times. At present it includes as board members two Nobel laureates, Douglass North and Vernon Smith, as well as chairman William Hume, president Gary Walton, and other leading academic and business leaders.

Finally, I thank five people who carefully reviewed and made constructive substantive suggestions: Joseph Bast, president of the Heartland Institute, whose board I chair; my friend Steven Graubart; Robin LaSota of the Academic Development Institute; the Cato Institute's Andrew Coulson; and an anonymous reviewer, all of whom informed me about relevant research that had escaped my attention. Perhaps needless to say, the remaining opinions, errors, and infelicities are solely my own.

Herbert J. Walberg
Chicago, IL

1. Introduction and Overview

U.S. Schools Are Falling Behind

The United States of America is arguably the world leader in income, wealth, military power, and cultural influence. It hovers near the top of international rankings in higher education, scientific and medical discoveries, and the productivity of many of its industries. Yet U.S. schools are behind those of most other economically advanced countries in both effectiveness and efficiency.[1] By the end of high school, U.S. academic achievement lags behind that of most member countries of the Organization for Economic Cooperation and Development—a group that includes most of the world's economically advanced countries.

In addition to being ineffective, American public schools are inefficient or unproductive, which is to say they get little return on taxpayers' dollars. Their per student costs rank among the top two or three countries in recent OECD surveys and have risen substantially over the last few decades. This pattern of low and declining efficiency is at odds with most other American enterprises, in which competition has generally led to improved quality and declining (inflation-adjusted) costs.

By widely accepted standards of what educated citizens should know, U.S. students perform poorly in civics, geography, history, and other subjects. Compared to students in other countries, older American students do poorly in mathematics, science, and foreign languages. Yet American students are not behind in the earliest years of schooling. Their achievement, relative to students in other countries, declines during the years when learning is chiefly the responsibility of schools. Indeed, the "value-added" gains in reading, mathematics, and science for American students are generally among the worst of students living in affluent countries. These findings are becoming better known to the public, parents, and legislators.

1

The latest available data indicate that the percentage of schools "in need of improvement" under the generally low standards imposed by states and the federal No Child Left Behind Act of 2002 has increased from 13 percent to 17 percent.[2] They and sharply increasing numbers of other schools face escalating sanctions, such as having to inform parents that their children are in failing schools, being required to allow parents to transfer their children to successful schools, replacing staff, and, if failure continues, possible closure.

Despite such present and prospective sanctions, despite widespread recognition of the achievement problem, despite higher school spending, the National Assessment of Educational Progress (referred to as "the nation's report card") reported in February 2007 that reading achievement of American 12th grade students had declined from 1992 through 2005. Standards, instead of rising, have declined; despite the drop in students' performance, teachers are giving them higher grades.[3]

Poor high school performance leads to poor college performance. According to the National Center for Public Policy and Higher Education, only 68 percent of ninth graders graduate on time; only 40 percent enroll directly in college.[4] Of high school seniors who took the American College Test for admission to college in 2006, only 51 percent met the college-readiness benchmark for reading. Of those who failed the reading benchmark, 84 percent also failed the mathematics benchmark, and 95 percent failed the science benchmark. Sorting the results by racial-ethnic groups, 59 percent of whites passed, as did 54 percent of Asians, 36 percent of Native Americans, 33 percent of Hispanics, and 21 percent of African Americans.[5] As a consequence of such poor preparation, some one million full-time freshmen enter colleges and universities each year, but fewer than 4 in 10 finish in four years, and only 6 in 10 finish in six years.[6]

> Because of poor prior preparation in high school, college graduates perform poorly: This past August [2006], the National Commission on the Future of Higher Education reported that "the quality of student learning—as measured by assessments of college graduates—is declining." It cited a stunning finding of the National Assessment of Adult Literacy: Only 31 percent of college-educated Americans qualify as "prose literate," meaning that at they can fully comprehend something as simple as a newspaper story. This number has shrunk from 40 percent a decade ago, apparently because the flood of badly educated new graduates is dragging down the average.[7]

In addition to being ineffective and inefficient, schools can be dangerous places, particularly those in big cities and those serving predominantly poor and minority students. In a recent poll, 73 percent of low-income parents and 46 percent of higher-income parents said they worried "a lot" about their children's exposure to drugs and alcohol at school. Similarly, 65 percent of low-income parents and 39 percent of higher-income parents worried a great deal about their children being assaulted or even kidnapped.[8]

Declining Productivity

U.S. citizens pay more per student for K–12 public education than nearly all other economically advanced countries, and the real (inflation-adjusted) per student costs of that schooling have increased substantially over the last several decades. Additional value is normally expected for additional money, but rising spending hasn't helped American schools to achieve more.[9]

The productivity of schools in the United States—the ratio of achievement to spending—is necessarily declining since achievement (the numerator) remains relatively low and spending (the denominator) is rising. It is costing more and more to get similar or worse results. According to research conducted by Harvard University economist Caroline Hoxby, the productivity of public schools in the United States fell between 55 and 73 percent between 1970–71 and 1998–99.[10]

This ratio underestimates the decline in school productivity because it does not take into account the rise in average scores on intelligence tests designed to measure children's capacity to succeed in school. This increase is attributable to better nutrition and housing and to rising levels of income, wealth, and intellectual stimulation at home in the last three decades. Productivity should have improved even if the schools did nothing different.[11]

Academic achievement matters because a country's achievement test scores in mathematics and science are strongly correlated with and predictive of a country's economic growth. Economic growth, in turn, is linked to objective measures of a country's quality of life in such fields as health, housing, and child rearing.[12] Thus, poor U.S. achievement test scores are not merely of academic interest. They have real-world consequences for the welfare of millions of children and young adults. Poor schools even threaten older generations

3

whose Social Security and pensions depend on a healthy economy and well-educated workforce.

These problems and prospects have not escaped the notice of employers and citizens. A national Conference Board survey polled 431 employers of recently hired high school and college graduates in 2006 and concluded that they generally lacked requisite general knowledge and basic skills of reading comprehension and mathematical computation. Graduates also generally lacked important skills in communication, collaboration, and critical thinking. [13] Perhaps as a consequence, only 3 in 10 voters in a 2006 national exit poll expected their children to enjoy a better standard of living than they do, contrary to much of the American experience of the past.[14]

International Talent Competition

Modern economies pay huge premiums for advanced, often specialized, knowledge and skills, or "high levels of human capital."[15] Such capital, which can apply to all areas of life, constitutes a vast and growing fraction of the value of modern firms and other organizations. As *The Economist* notes:

> The value of "intangible" assets—everything from skilled workers to patents to know-how—has ballooned from 20% of the value of companies in the S&P 500 to 70% today. The proportion of American workers doing jobs that call for complex skills [has] thus grown three times as fast as employment in general. As other economies move in the same direction, the global demand is rising quickly.... The imminent retirement of the baby-boomers means that companies will lose large numbers of experienced workers in a short space of time.... By one count half the top people at America's 500 leading companies will go in the next five years.[16]

As Table 1-1 shows, higher levels of human capital indicated by education levels are strongly associated with wages. Workers with advanced professional degrees, for example, earned wages more than five times those of workers who didn't finish high school. Only those with the highest levels of education—those with master's degrees in business administration and those with doctorates in academic scholarship, law, and medicine—averaged higher inflation-adjusted wage gains from 2001 through 2005. Unlike past generations, most workers actually lost rather than gained in real wage

4

Table 1-1
AVERAGE WAGES AND INCREASES IN WAGES AMONG AMERICAN WAGE EARNERS

Education	Average Wages, 2005	Percent Change, 2001–2005
Didn't finish high school	$ 22,274	−4.6
High school graduate	31,665	−0.2
Some college	38,009	−2.5
College graduate	56,740	−3.1
Master's	68,302	−1.8
Ph.D.	93,593	2.9
MBA, JD, MD	119,343	10.6

SOURCE: Current Population Survey.

NOTES: "Some college" includes associate arts degrees that, in principle, require two years of college work. "Percent change" is inflation adjusted.

income.[17] The growth of national and international competition, particularly from rising East and South Asia, as well as the Internet and other new media, allows more highly educated "superstars" in business, finance, law, entertainment, sports, and other fields to exercise their specialized talents more widely and remuneratively— often in organizations with worldwide reach. Their wages and other income often rise rapidly. In short, on average, the highly educated and rich get richer.

Attaining high levels of education and income usually requires strong K–12 preparation.[18] Those without advanced mathematics (including calculus) in high school are unlikely to succeed in the hard sciences or engineering. Those without strong verbal skills are unlikely to succeed in law. Without a solid core of basic knowledge and skills, and without the capacity and discipline for hard, focused study built up in the early years, students are unlikely to succeed in later education and in advanced careers (though, of course, there are exceptions such as Oracle's Larry Ellison, Microsoft's Bill Gates, and Apple's Steve Jobs, none of whom graduated from college).

Both individuals and countries with advanced school-acquired human capital have benefited enormously, particularly in the last few decades, as free markets have taken better hold beyond North America and Western Europe. The OECD, for example, reported

5

trends in schooling among its affluent member countries and found that education in East Asia continues rapidly to expand and improve. Two decades ago, South Korea was one of the poorest education performers. Today, its high school students, on average, outscore most of those in other economically advanced countries in mathematics and science.

Among the main industrialized countries, moreover, Korea ranks first in the percentage of high school completers between the ages of 25 and 34—97 percent. The head of the Education Indicators and Analysis division of the OECD, Andreas Schleicher, observed, "Tomorrow's high-skilled jobs in innovation and R&D—and the high wages that go with them—will be relocated in Asia unless the European Union and the U.S. make significant progress."[19]

The consequences of East Asia's higher standards and graduation rates are already substantially apparent. According to *The Economist*, "The real driver of the world economy has been Asia, which has accounted for over half of the world's growth since 2001" [through 2005] in contrast to America's contribution of only 13 percent of the growth.[20]

The benefits of strong K–12 education systems are not restricted to individual and national income. Higher achievement appears to reduce child and adult mortality[21] and to improve health throughout the lifespan.[22]

American Immigrants

The American economy has long benefited from the immigration of talented and ambitious people. Today, the highest levels of economically and technologically significant U.S. talent are often found among immigrants rather than American-born workers. Half of the Nobel Prizes that went to Americans, for example, were awarded to immigrants; more than half of the Ph.D.s working in America are immigrants; and "a quarter of Silicon Valley companies were started by Indians and Chinese."[23]

But the United States may not be able to depend on continuing talent immigration. A survey of international firms showed that between 25 and 82 percent planned to increase the amount of research and development they conduct in China and India in automotive engineering, consumer products, information technology, media and entertainment, industrial goods, telecommunications, and financial services.[24]

Missing their families or seeing opportunity back home, talented immigrants are now more likely to return. Returnees from America, for example, founded 3 in 10 of Taiwan's new companies.[25] Lower labor costs in developing countries serve as magnets. Indian college graduates are paid roughly 12 percent of the salaries earned by their American counterparts. Because Indians, on average, also work longer hours than Americans, firms can "buy almost ten Indian brains for the price of one American one."[26]

For these and other reasons, the once dominant old-line U.S. unionized industries have steadily declined. The percentage of employed wage and salary workers who are members of unions declined from 20.1 to 14.0 percent from 1983 to 2005 (although 4 in 10 government workers were unionized in 2005).[27] In January 2006 General Motors reported its largest annual loss in more than a decade in the face of competition from Asia and falling sales. In a watershed moment in the same year, GM was finally eclipsed by Toyota as the world's number-one automaker after a 40-year decline in its market share.

Similarly, Chrysler was forced to merge with (German) Daimler-Benz, and Bill Ford now faces the prospect of presiding over the bankruptcy of his eponymous company. Long bound by tough union contracts, Ford declared, "From now on, our products will be designed and built to satisfy the customer, not just to fill a factory."[28] (Apparently, when all else fails, customers are considered.)

All this goes to show that American citizens face increased international competition. They cannot depend on the major industries that formerly led the world to continue without a well-educated workforce. Nor can they depend on immigrants or the present K–12 school system to save the day without effective reforms.

School Choice

Because high levels of knowledge and skill increasingly determine individual and national success, Americans and others are keenly interested in changes in schools that may be effective in increasing youngsters' achievement. Opinion polls, discussed in subsequent chapters, show that majorities of adults are concerned about low school standards and student achievement levels. Parents are particularly concerned. Thanks to the spread of "school report cards" and the disclosure required by states and the federal No Child Left Behind Act, more parents than ever before are aware that their children are attending failing schools. This information is changing the terms of the national debate over school reform.

Strong majorities of parents favor programs that enable parents to choose the schools, public or private, that their children attend, with public funding following the student. Parents also favor holding schools accountable for results. A majority of parents say they would send their children to private schools if they could afford the tuition. And, perhaps a sign of growing dissatisfaction with public schools, a large and growing number of parents are homeschooling their children. About 1.2 million children, or 2 percent of age-eligible youngsters, are currently homeschooled.

Discontent with public schools is reflected in most states' legislation and efforts to expand school choice, but these efforts have been fought, usually successfully, by public school boards, teachers' unions, and administrators and their allies. The federal No Child Left Behind Act and new laws in a growing number of states require authorities to give students in repeatedly failing public schools the choice of transferring to other public or private schools. Even though states and districts often evade this requirement, enrollment in voucher, education tax credit, and charter school programs is growing rapidly, though from relatively small numbers, in cities across the country.

Because of the growing interest in school choice and its importance for public policy and the nation's future, this book assesses a broad range of school choice outcomes, focusing particularly on achievement test performance, costs, and parental and public opinion. It also brings together research on "market effects," that is, the effects that competition from charter schools, voucher programs, and private schools as a whole have on traditional public schools.

This book gives little attention to homeschooling or tax credits for tuition and other expenses, since little rigorous, empirical research is available to assess their effects. Readers interested in these and related topics may find the following references useful starting points: the history of school choice from ancient to modern times,[29] private school choice in foreign countries,[30] analysis of various forms and degrees of choice,[31] and legislative principles for school choice.[32]

Measurable Outcomes

A major focus of this book is on standardized achievement tests, even though such tests do not represent the sum of students' knowledge, attitudes, and skills or capture a host of other outcomes expected from education. They are, however, America's and other countries' academic currency. Standardized achievement tests are the most common measure used to assess school performance across all 50 states and the chief indicator of progress of state legislation and the No Child Left Behind Act. The public supports more extensive test use, wider reporting of results, and accountability for progress.

Early academic test results are reasonably accurate predictors of students' success in later grades, retention in school, and college admission (even to elite universities). No one has shown that high achievement scores deter critical thinking, ethical behavior, or other valuable outcomes; rather the opposite appears to be evident: greater knowledge is likely to help people make better decisions, contribute more to society, and lead desirable lives.

Even so, academic achievement is not the only outcome that may be valuable to all the parties who participate in the K–12 education process. Some schools are greatly oversubscribed while others sit half empty: Parents, by their choices, are signaling which schools they believe are doing the better job. Similarly, surveys show that parents who send their children to private schools or charter schools are more satisfied than parents who have not made a choice. In free societies, consumer opinion about schools is an important consideration, just as it is in other areas of life.

In addition to achievement and consumer opinion, other measures of school success are reported here when available. These include high school and college graduation rates and students' voluntary charitable activities in school and later adult life. Because of the American problem of low public school cost-effectiveness, the costs of choice schools and traditional public schools are also considered.

Credibility and Selection of Evidence

This book sets aside philosophical controversies about school choice and confines itself largely to empirical research on its effects. Some research on this topic is set aside since it does not measure up to modern social science research standards. Opinion research counts for little, for example, unless results are obtained from surveys of large, well-defined populations or large, random samples of them. Expert observers' observations may be subjective and merely confirm presuppositions. The rampant anecdotalism common in many public discussions of school choice cannot be trusted and is ignored here, even though it is often highly influential in both policy and practice.

Perhaps the most difficult problem in evaluating school choice research is estimating causal effects. It is often said, and just as often ignored, in policy discussions that correlation does not mean causation. The research selected for discussion in this book is largely confined to several types regarded as scientific in the applied fields such as medicine, epidemiology, agriculture, engineering, psychology, and increasingly in education and the social sciences. With illustrations, these may be simply and nontechnically defined as follows:

- "Randomized field trials," the gold standard of causality, compare the academic achievement and other measurable outcomes of admitted applicants to an oversubscribed voucher program or charter school with those of unadmitted applicants who attended the traditional public school. Since whether any applicant is admitted or not is determined by lottery, any "statistically significant" difference between the two groups of students is most likely attributable to the effectiveness of the "treatment," in this case the type of school chosen, rather than chance.
- "Quasi-experiments" in which students have not been randomly assigned to schools, but statistical adjustments, usually based on achievement pretests, are made in an effort to remove preexisting differences among students before they enrolled in choice and other schools. In the hope that these adjustments eliminate possible "selection biases," investigators compare the outcome results of students in choice and other schools.
- "Correlational analyses" (usually regression analyses), more often employed by economists than other scholars, compare non-randomly-assigned students in two or more groups of schools by statistically controlling for preexisting differences among students including achievement, race, socioeconomic status, and other characteristics.

These methods of research deserve further discussion here. The social sciences—anthropology, economics, political science, and sociology—are perhaps a half-century behind the applied natural and human sciences in drawing the causal inferences necessary to base policy and practice decisions on scientific conclusions. Random assignment of units to experimental and control or contrast conditions (or treatments) is now generally required in agronomy, medicine, public health, and the rigorous parts of psychology and educational research. Experiments require that the units of analysis be randomly assigned to alternative conditions purely by chance, for example, a coin flip (or, usually, randomly generated numbers). Thus, there is no reason to think that groups initially differ (though this possibility should be investigated rather than assumed).

The difference in outcomes can be straightforwardly assessed with a far smaller set of assumptions than required in nonexperimental research (such as that the groups have indeed been subjected to the specified conditions, which can be investigated). Experimental studies do not require the usually disputable and often ideological questions about specifying, controlling for, and reliably measuring *all* other causes. In contrast, social scientists have come to conflicting conclusions from the same data, depending on social scientists' initial causal views, which are often assumed rather than probed.

Because a student's academic achievement prior to moving to a different school often accounts for the bulk of variations in later test scores, studies with measures of achievement gains from one occasion to another (or more than two occasions) are given special weight in this book. Measuring value-added gains or "over-time" growth in achievement during intervening periods increases the sensitivity of the study, reduces possible biases attributable to preexisting differences among students, and thus makes the findings more creditable. Such prior information helps to take into account the powerful influence of families and measures the separate and distinct contribution of the school to a student's achievement.

Other things being equal, "cross-sectional" studies of scores obtained on only one occasion as well as studies that follow grouped rather than individual students' progress are much less credible, and only a few are discussed in this book in cases in which no individual value-added, learning-gain research is available. Once again, with other things being equal, large, randomly chosen samples of large, well-defined populations (preferably a state or nation) allow correspondingly more general causal inferences than small samples within a single community or city.

Social and educational research involves many plausible variables and difficult measurement and sampling problems. Any study is likely to have several flaws. Therefore, scholars in such professions as medicine and psychology weight findings more heavily that replicate, that is, repeat the same findings, preferably many times in a variety of circumstances. This book describes the methods and findings of particularly rigorous studies, but it also draws on previous summaries of many studies on a number of topics. These are called "reviews of research" since they critically evaluate multiple studies and point out findings that are consistent across them.

Unlike news accounts, they avoid putting exclusive weight on a single study when other studies are also available. They also provide a better indication of whether an effect is broadly found in many circumstances by several investigators rather than by only a single study that may be flawed in known and unknown ways.

On some topics, studies that do not meet the above standards may shed light on causality. An example is studies of economically advanced and developing countries that rapidly and substantially introduced vouchers, and for which investigators have documented massive changes in test scores; private school enrollments; and integration of immigrant, special needs, and minority students. In one case discussed, a randomized experimental trial was employed to test the effects of school choice on achievement. Of course, there remains the question of whether such findings can be generalized to the United States and to other countries. In addition to studies of massive national changes, systematic observational studies of chosen schools that have had outstanding success may be reasonable to review to see what sets those schools apart from other schools.

This book draws on the largest body of rigorous evidence the author could amass on school choice and competitive effects. Admittedly, no single study or piece of evidence is definitive. The situation may be likened to the search for "dose-response" connections between cigarette smoking and lung cancer. Many (regression) studies revealed the correlational linkage between the two after "controlling for" (or statistically taking into account) age, poverty, ethnicity, ambient air pollution, and other things thought to be associated with lung cancer.

These correlational findings were consistent with multiple experimental studies of laboratory animals randomly chosen to be exposed and unexposed to large "doses" of tobacco smoke. These multiple, multimethod, multisample studies in wide-ranging conditions enabled analysts to arrive at a decisive conclusion on the otherwise elusive health effects of cigarette smoking. Similarly, given the problems of evaluating social programs, the key consideration adopted here is the robustness, or consistency, of findings in many widely differing circumstances since any given study is likely to have possibly vitiating flaws.

Caveat

Much of the evidence assembled here concerns averages of achievement test scores and other outcomes for choice and traditional public schools. Even large differences in averages of any two school types, however, should not be taken as indicating that all of the schools of one type are better than all those of another. Undoubtedly, most private and traditional schools either underperform or overperform the averages for their types, and achievement by the two types of schools should be expected to overlap to a greater or lesser extent. Charter schools, for example, are heterogeneous because they were conceived as a way to promote diversity, innovation, and productivity. Some charter schools focus on at-risk or gifted students, others on pregnant teens, and still others are built around a particular educational philosophy or curriculum (such as the academically focused Core Knowledge program).

Despite such variation, statistically significant differences, expressed as averages, between charter and traditional schools are not to be dismissed. It is important if the average student in one type of choice school does better or worse than the average student in another type of school. Since student scores from lowest to highest in the two types of schools contribute to overall averages, they are the most useful, and therefore the most commonly used, indicator of group characteristics and differences among groups.

Still, in some instances, investigators have found distinctive effects on some kinds of students. When these special effects are consistent across studies, they are worth noting.

A Taxonomy of School Choice

Table 1-2 shows a simplified breakdown of the possible school governance and funding combinations. Starting in the upper-right

Table 1-2
CATEGORIES OF SCHOOL FUNDING AND OPERATION

Government Funded \ Government Operated	Yes	No (or contracted out by the state)
No	N/A	Self-schooling Homeschooling For-profit tutoring and schooling Private independent and sectarian schools Early American locally controlled schools
Yes	Traditional public schools	Charter schools

category is an example of perhaps the most private form of education, self-schooling, exemplified by the famous autodidact Abraham Lincoln. Second, some 1.25 million youngsters, now schooled at home, represent strong and rising preferences for nongovernment schooling.

Continuing in the upper-right quadrant, when families think they lack the knowledge, skills, time, or desire to pursue homeschooling, yet want things that public schools do not adequately provide, they may voluntarily choose to pay for private tutoring. East Asia's thriving private tutoring sector is widely credited for at least a part of that region's top scores on international achievement tests, and tutoring services are also popular with East Asian immigrants to the United States, who also tend to be highly successful students.

An interesting example is Korea, which has a $15 billion per year, highly competitive for-profit *hagwon* tutoring industry with extensive brick-and-mortar facilities. Since 2000, however, the firm Megastudy has been offering Web-based educational services and now boasts 2,000 courses. Teachers receive about a quarter of the subscription income to their lectures, which has added up to a payment of $2 million in the case of one charismatic English teacher in a single recent year.[33] Such entrepreneurship and differential pay are nearly unheard of in Western public and private schools. Indeed, the lack of entrepreneurship and incentives may be a major reason for the low and declining productivity of K–12 education.

For-profit companies have begun to supply schooling in the United States and other countries.[34] A little research on their effectiveness is available, but much of it has been carried out or sponsored by the firms themselves or by teachers' unions, which are often hostile toward for-profit competition and choice in general. The research, moreover, does not meet the standards of studies summarized here. For this reason, the effects of self-schooling, home-schooling, and for-profit schooling are not summarized here.

Private schools, both independent and sectarian, are another choice. Many provide both academic and religious instruction. They may be not only more pleasing to parents but also more cost-effective and time efficient than homeschooling since a single teacher may have responsibility for a dozen to three dozen students, freeing parents' time.

As is explained in Chapter 4, we may think of "traditional" public schools as the American way, that is, owned, funded, and operated by the government. But for the first two centuries of American history, nearly all schools were either fully private or locally organized public/private hybrid institutions. Citizens in tiny communities paid for and controlled their own schools, including one-room country schools. These schools assimilated tens of millions of English- and non-English-speaking immigrants into American society, and they became strong contributors to the economy and society. Tiny school districts in low population density states such as Montana, enrolling between one and few hundred students, still retain highly localized control and typically have among the highest achievement test scores.

Since around 1925, however, consolidation has collapsed roughly 115,000 separate school districts into about 15,000, and average school size has risen by a factor of five. This consolidation has greatly worsened parents' prospects for influencing the boards of their children's schools through school board elections. Political scientists refer to "voter dilution" as the comparatively weak weight of a citizen's vote in a large city compared to one in a village.

Increased centralization, moreover, has produced school boards less well informed about the day-to-day operations of schools. Chicago Public School Board members, for example, could probably not name the more than 500 schools within their purview. Unlike students of yesteryear who went to private or nearly private locally controlled schools, most students today go to schools in large centralized districts, heavily regulated by state and federal government rather than governed by citizens in small school communities surrounding the school.

Charter schools are government-funded and government-supervised institutions whose management is directed by private boards. Although they are intended to offer greater parental choice and educational diversity, subsequent chapters document the often heavy regulatory and other burdens imposed on them, such as requirements to hire union employees and administer state tests and per pupil funding that is limited, on average, to about 80 percent of that received by traditional public schools.

Charter boards may appoint their own staffs or hire nonprofit or for-profit management organizations. The extent to which they are freed from conventional public school regulations varies substantially from state to state, but in all cases charter schools are accountable to their chartering authority, often the local school district, state, or state-appointed charter issuer, for student achievement and progress and are subject to closure for poor performance or insufficient enrollment.

Overview of Chapters

The remaining chapters focus primarily on the effects of the major types of school choice. Chapter 2 examines charter school studies. Chapter 3 describes research on the effects of vouchers, which are scholarships that state and local authorities, for-profit and nonprofit organizations, and individuals give directly to families to enable them to send their children to the private schools of their choice. The U.S. Supreme Court ruled in 2002 that parents of public school children, when granted vouchers, can enroll their children in parochial schools, provided that is the parents' choice. Cleveland, Milwaukee, Washington, DC, and Florida have publicly funded vouchers. The Utah legislature recently passed a statewide voucher bill, which is to eventually serve all K–12 students. Nonpublic organizations and individuals in about 50 cities provide private vouchers, mostly for poor and minority children to attend parochial and nonsectarian independent schools. Parents in several states have sought vouchers as a form of legal relief from repeatedly failing public schools (most recently, in New Jersey and Atlanta, Georgia).

Chapter 4 describes private schools, which generally fall into one of two categories, each of which has several names that are taken as synonymous here: (1) independent or nonsectarian and (2) religious, sectarian, or parochial. While private schools are largely funded and governed privately, they are government regulated to some extent and may in the United States receive small amounts of public funds for such things as transportation, tutoring, and children in poverty. This chapter has little to say about for-profit schools and home-schooling, since research on them does not meet the standards mentioned above. Both types of private schooling are very interesting, nevertheless, and over time may have valuable lessons to teach.

Chapter 5 summarizes the effects of school choice on the achievement of all students within a given geopolitical area (such as a city or state). Although some educators fear competitors would lure only the best students from underperforming public schools, and lower average achievement in public schools, economists might predict the opposite: that competition would enhance performance, efficiency, and consumer satisfaction in public as well as private schools. The ways to test this idea include examining whether the presence of many private schools in a city or county is positively correlated with test scores in traditional public schools, whether countries that rapidly introduce vouchers nationwide see better performance and satisfaction, and whether those countries see increased socioeconomic isolation of students or for-profit firms taking advantage of ill-informed immigrant parents. Such plausible ideas should be put to factual test.

Chapter 6 analyzes recent national public opinion polls about public and private schools and privatization policies as well as school-specific surveys of charter and voucher parents. Since schools are to serve society or the public in general and parents in particular, it would seem reasonable to ask the public and parents. As documented in Chapter 6, surveys reveal that the public has strong opinions about school competition, funding, and accountability; and parents often have similarly intense opinions about their own children's schools. To gain an understanding of choice and market effects, these views and opinions need to be taken into account.

Chapter 7 gathers the themes from the foregoing chapters, each with its separate sources of evidence. It summarizes general conclusions that seem warranted from the most rigorous research.

2. Charter School Effects

Charter schools have multiplied rapidly in the United States as a result of parental demand and state legislation.[1] The first charter schools opened in Minnesota in 1992, and as of 2006 there were roughly 4,000 operating in 40 states and the District of Columbia, enrolling about one million students. This chapter assembles the most rigorous evidence on six different aspects of charter schools:

- their popularity,
- their performance relative to traditional government schools,
- the achievement gains of their students,
- their effect on achievement in nearby traditional public schools,
- public and parental knowledge and opinions about them, and
- the regulatory and funding problems faced by the charter school sector.

Charter School Popularity

One characteristic of charter schools is not in dispute—parents favor them over traditional public schools. Nationwide, charter school waiting lists contain nearly 9 percent of the number of students currently enrolled in the charter sector. In nine states, the number of students on waiting lists exceeds 20 percent of charter school enrollment. Demand is highest in Massachusetts, where waitlists total approximately 55 percent of total charter enrollment, followed by Connecticut, where the figure approaches 50 percent.[2] The waiting lists might be even longer if more parents knew about charters. This pent-up demand is due, in part, to the fact that many states cap the total number of charter schools that can be created, limit access on the basis of place of residence, and/or cap the number of students that any school can enroll.

In Chicago, for example, charter schools are extraordinarily oversubscribed. A recent Progressive Policy Institute study[3] showed that all but 1 of the city's 27 charter campuses (some schools have multiple campuses) had more applicants than open spaces available. Nine of the campuses had three times as many applicants as seats, and at one school the ratio was 10 to 1.

Charter schools currently serve 3.6 percent of the Chicago student population, which means that comparatively few students have access to their programs. The demand for alternatives to ineffective traditional public schools isn't difficult to fathom: according to a report by the Illinois Facilities Fund, only 16 percent of the city's high school students and barely one-half of Chicago's elementary students have access to effective schools.[4] Although the analysis is not causally rigorous (see subsequent sections for studies that are), the information that may concern parents is that all the charter high schools outperformed the average scores of the traditional public schools that their students would have otherwise attended.[5] Seven of 10 Chicago charter elementary schools improved faster than traditional Chicago public schools.

One reason charter schools are so popular is that, according to national surveys, the majority of parents would send their children to private schools if the cost of tuition were not an issue.[6] African-American parents feel particularly strongly about this; a nationally estimated 89 percent would send their children to private schools if tuition were provided.[7] Publicly funded charter schools, since they are privately governed and operated, are naturally appealing to parents who prefer semiprivate to state-run schools.

Charter schools are also popular because individual schools that fail to please parents will fail to attract students and as a result can be forced to close. Public schools that fail to please parents continue nevertheless to have students assigned to them and remain open year after year. Whether the No Child Left Behind Act and state legislation will actually improve or close failing traditional public schools remains to be seen.

Parental satisfaction is important but often overlooked in the school choice debate. Many experts seem to believe that only academic test scores are "objective" or important measures of school quality, while the views of parents and citizens are subjective or even irrelevant. Both these beliefs are incorrect, as will be shown later in this chapter and in subsequent chapters. A nation that depends on individual choice and responsibility in so many other areas of economic and social life should not dismiss consumer opinions in education. Measuring parents' satisfaction with different types of schools is a way to ensure that their views are not overlooked.

20

Academic Achievement of Charter Schools

Well-designed studies increasingly show that charter schools, on average, produce academic achievement levels that exceed those of traditional pubic schools, even though most charter schools are less than five years old and operate with substantially less funding than do traditional public schools.

Single-Point-in-Time Studies

The most comprehensive single-point-in-time study of charter schools was conducted by Harvard University economist Caroline Hoxby.[8] She analyzed data from 99 percent of the nation's charter schools. Hoxby's study is a straightforward comparison of achievement rather than achievement gains, but it has the huge advantage of including data for essentially all the charter schools in the nation and nearby traditional public schools.

Using state-mandated test data, Hoxby found:

> Compared to students in the matched public school, charter students are 5.2 percent more likely to be proficient in reading and 3.2 percent more likely to be proficient in math on their state's exams. Charter schools that have been in operation longer have a greater proficiency advantage over the matched public schools. For example, in reading, the advantage is 2.5 percent for a charter school that has been operating 1 to 4 years, 5.2 percent for a school operating 5 to 8 years, and 10.1 percent for a school operating 9 to 11 years.[9]

Hoxby found the largest differences in proficiency levels in states where charter schools were most common. For example, compared to students attending matched traditional public schools, Alaska's charter students were about 20 percent more likely to be proficient in reading and math, Arizona's about 10 percent more likely to be proficient in both disciplines, and California's 9 percent more likely to be proficient in reading and 5 percent more likely to be proficient in math.[10]

Hoxby's results suggest that poor and Hispanic students performed well in charter schools and show that they accounted for a higher percentage of charter than of traditional public school enrollments. Another important finding of Hoxby's study is that charter school students were "more likely to have a proficiency advantage if their state has a strong charter school law that gives the schools autonomy and that ensures that charter schools get a substantial fraction of the total per-pupil funding of traditional public schools."[11]

Hoxby found that in large urban school districts with high levels of choice, charter schools were 35 percent more likely to have curricula with rigorous core requirements in English, mathematics, social studies, science, and foreign language.[12] Schools of choice in these districts also demonstrated more structured classrooms, heightened attention to academic discipline, and greater use of student standardized test results to evaluate administrative performance. Research shows these conditions yield higher achievement.[13]

Finally, Hoxby also reported that charter school students are more likely to have relatively higher achievement than traditional school students if their state enacted a charter law early. Top-performing states for charter schools, with early charter school law enactment dates, are Arizona, 1994; California, 1992; Colorado, 1993; the District of Columbia, 1996; Hawaii, 1994; Illinois, 1996; Louisiana, 1995; and Massachusetts, 1993. On average, states with charter school laws enacted them in 1996, but 10 states have no charter law yet. States that enacted their laws early tend to be more likely to provide more adequate funding, more autonomy, multiple chartering authorities, and other benefits to charter schools, which appear to be the reasons their charter schools achieve better outcomes than traditional schools in their states.[14]

Thus, the largest single-point-in-time study ever carried out suggests that charter schools exceeded traditional schools in achievement, that poor and Hispanic students do especially well in them, and that outcomes improve as charter schools gain experience and are given more autonomy and funding levels closer to those of traditional public schools.

Two other more recent single-point-in-time studies of charter schools appeared to contradict Hoxby's findings. The first, by the American Federation of Teachers—the nation's second-largest teachers' union—received front-page coverage in the *New York Times* when released in August 2004.[15] The AFT used National Assessment of Educational Progress scores to compare the achievement of students in traditional and charter schools. A second study, by the National Center for Education Statistics, also used NAEP results to allegedly confirm the AFT's findings.[16] Both studies claimed to find that African-American and Latino students in charter schools performed as well as their peers in traditional public schools, but that charter school students eligible for free lunch and those in urban areas underperformed their peers in district-run public schools.

These studies are unlikely to be reliable because they are both based on small samples of charter schools that were unmatched and not comparable to nearby traditional schools. The National Assessment surveys only about 3 percent of all schools, and charter schools are only a small percentage of this already small sample. Such small samples, moreover, are not designed to compare achievement of choice schools with that of traditional public schools and are likely to be misleading.

Reviews of Research

Hoxby's national charter school study is one of 44 studies of U.S. charter school achievement included in Bryan Hassel's review of the literature, the most comprehensive such review to date.[17] Hassel aptly cautions against causal inferences about charter school effectiveness from single-point-in-time studies and bases his conclusions largely on studies that trace changes in individual students' performance over time. Since students' achievement in school is substantially affected by nonschool factors, differences among students at a single point in time should not be attributed completely or even substantially to their present schools. That would be analogous to comparing the completion times of runners who started at different locations.

Nor can preexisting differences among students be validly adjusted away by questionnaire indicators of such things as enduring family socioeconomic status based on student impressions of the parents' income, occupation, and education, particularly among younger children and those who have undergone changing family circumstances such as a job loss or the death of a parent. Federal Title 1 poverty status (used to assign subsidized federally sponsored lunches) divides children into poor and nonpoor groups, but this dichotomy lacks precision and may also vary across youngsters' lives. Some families, moreover, don't report their incomes to school authorities since it might stigmatize them or because they think it is a private matter. For such reasons, Hassel singled out the 26 most rigorous causal studies, those that followed students and schools over time to measure their comparative progress. Of these 26 rigorous studies, he found that

23

- 12 concluded that overall gains in charter schools were larger than those in other public schools;
- 4 concluded that charter schools' gains were higher in certain significant categories of schools, such as elementary schools, high schools, or schools serving at-risk students;
- 6 concluded that there were comparable gains in charter and traditional public schools; and
- 4 concluded that charter schools' overall gains lagged behind.

Thus, in 16 of the 26 rigorous studies, charter schools excelled traditional public schools.

Seven studies that Hassel reviewed examined whether charter schools improve their performance over time, since new schools usually face start-up challenges such as educating and evaluating new staff and developing and evaluating curricula. Five of the seven studies concluded that they do. Since most charter schools in the nation are relatively new, their performance in the coming years can be expected to improve and further outpace that of traditional public schools.

Three Exemplary Over-Time Studies

Three longitudinal studies (those that measure changes in an attribute over time) provide examples of more rigorous research and yield particular insights on the effects of charter schools.[18] Greene, Forster, and Winters provide an extensive analysis of student achievement data over a one-year period in 11 states. Charter schools performed better than nearby public schools on mathematics tests by three percentile points and in reading by two percentile points; both of these results were statistically significant at high levels.[19]

An extensive study of charter schools in Arizona by Solomon and Goldschmidt[20] challenges the notion that charter school achievement is attributable to bias in admitting only superior students (which would be against charter laws in most cases since charter schools can generally select applicants only by lottery and then only if they are oversubscribed). The authors analyzed 157,671 test scores of 62,207 students attending 873 schools.

Solomon and Goldschmidt found that charter school students generally started off with lower achievement than their peers in traditional public schools, controlled for factors such as transferring schools, socioeconomic status, and not speaking English as a primary

24

language. Despite their initial achievement handicap, charter school students showed overall annual achievement growth approximately three points greater than that of their noncharter peers. Charter school students surpassed students in traditional public schools on the Stanford Achievement Tests in reading by the end of 12th grade. Solmon and Goldschmidt reported that the long-term benefits of switching to charter schools outweighed the short-term disruption when the transfer occurred before eighth grade.

A third longitudinal study, by Loveless, Kelly, and Henriques,[21] compared the achievement gains in 49 California schools from the four-year period, 1986–89, when they were traditional public schools, to 2001–04, after they were converted to charter schools. Enrollment data, demographic characteristics of students, and credentials and experience of teachers did not change during the conversion period, but achievement scores rose significantly. This study is particularly pertinent for education policy, given that the federal No Child Left Behind Act compels state authorities to consider, among other sanctions, converting failing traditional schools to charter schools or risk losing substantial federal funds.

A Random-Assignment Study

The Hoxby study discussed above made no claim for causally assessing effectiveness gains across time but cautiously answered the question: How do the achievement levels of nearly all charter schools and nearby traditional schools compare?

Hoxby subsequently collaborated with Jonah Rockoff[22] to produce the most rigorous random-assignment study of the effects of charter schools yet undertaken, using academic achievement data and the admission status of student applicants to the campuses of possibly the nation's largest charter school at the time, the Chicago International Charter School, which now has nine campuses. Since the school was oversubscribed, students were chosen by lottery either to be enrolled in the charter school or to remain in their traditional schools. Hoxby and Rockoff described their methodology as follows:

> Our treatment group (those who, in medicine, would receive the pill) comprises charter school applicants who drew a lottery number that earned them a place at one of the charter schools (lotteried in). Our control group (those who would receive the placebo) comprises the applicants who were lotteried out. All told, the study focuses on 2,448 students who

25

are divided between the lotteried-in and lotteried-out groups. It's important to realize that all of the students in the study applied to charter schools, so self-selection is the same for all of them. All that distinguishes the groups is their randomly drawn lottery numbers, so we can be confident that the groups are comparable not only in observable ways (like race and income), but also in less tangible ways, such as motivation to succeed. Currently, we can compare the progress of both groups for up to four years following their application. We are continuing the study and will report further results as they become available.[23]

Hoxby and Rockoff found that the charter campuses raised achievement by 5 to 6 points in mathematics and 6 points in reading for students who enrolled in the charter schools in grade five or earlier (too few students enrolled in the later grades to allow similar comparisons). The average student gained 2.5 to 3 extra points for each year at the charter school.

The achievement gains reported by Hoxby and Rockoff are large, equal to nearly half the achievement gap between the disadvantaged minority students and middle-income nonminority students. As Hoxby and Rockoff conclude, "If the students continued to make such gains for each year they spent in charter schools (a big 'if'), then the gap between the charter school students and their suburban counterparts would close entirely after about five years of school."[24]

Charter Schools in England

The Education Reform Act, adopted in 1988, offers all families in England and Wales the right to attend any government-run school, even if it is outside their tax community or district. School funding follows directly from student enrollment under a comprehensive nationwide school choice program.

Evaluations indicate high parental satisfaction with the program, and schools tend to operate with more autonomy and efficiency as a result of increased market competitiveness. According to Belfield and Levin's review, "schools are neither more nor less segregated according to ability, race, or socioeconomic status than they were prior to the reforms; and there is no evidence to show that some schools have degenerated substantially."[25]

Charter School Effects on Traditional Public Schools

In the *State of the Charter Movement 2005*, Gregg Vanourek noted wide variations in charter school "market shares" across states even though the enrollment in charter schools was low, about 2 percent of the nation's pupils.[26] This variation allows the study of "ripple" or "competitive" effects on public school systems in districts where charter schools are concentrated. A U.S. Government Accountability Office report concludes that each of the 49 districts in the study "changed the way it conducted its business and/or operations in response to charter schools. In 90 percent of the districts, leaders indicated they made changes in several areas of their district's operations in response to charter schools."[27]

Sixty-one percent of the districts in the GAO report said they changed their educational offerings, and 49 percent began at least one new educational program in traditional public schools. The report concluded that district responses to charter schools tend to evolve over time, and numerous factors affect districts' reactions to charter school competition, including how district and school leaders perceive charter schools, the "overall ecology of choice in the district," student performance, district enrollment trends, and whether charter schools generate significant media attention and community awareness.

Caroline Hoxby carried out pioneering research on this topic in 2002 with her analysis of the competitive effects of charter schools on conventional public schools in Michigan and Arizona, where traditional public schools faced losing at least 6 percent of student enrollment to charter schools. Hoxby studied how this competition affects traditional public school achievement. In Michigan, she found that student achievement in traditional public schools made "modest" improvements in response to competition from charter schools. In Arizona, the effect of charter school competition on traditional public school students was "similar to or just a bit larger than the gains made by Michigan public school students."[28] Her analysis of demographic patterns of students enrolled in charter schools compared with traditional public schools in Michigan and Arizona showed that charter schools do not "cream skim or reverse cream skim" in any consistent way. Conventional public schools and charter schools enrolled similar percentages of African-American students in Michigan and similar percentages of Latino students in Arizona.

27

When analyzing the change in achievement after a Michigan district is faced with charter school competition (at least 6 percent charter enrollment) between the years of 1992–93 and 1999–2000 on the Michigan Assessment of Educational Progress, Hoxby found: "Fourth-grade reading and math scores were, respectively, 1.21 and 1.11 scale points higher in schools that faced charter school competition after they began to face competition. Seventh-grade reading and math scores were, respectively, 1.37 and 0.96 scale points higher."[29] Hoxby points out that the traditional public schools faced with significant charter school competition in Michigan raised achievement relative to their own previous levels of performance and to that of other Michigan schools not subjected to competition from charter schools.

In Arizona, which is considered to have highly favorable legislation for charter schools, traditional public schools raised achievement when charter school competition reached critical thresholds. By 1999–2000, charter school enrollment reached 5.3 percent, the highest in any American state. Using methods similar to those used to study differences in achievement in Michigan, Hoxby found: "Achievement rose by 2.31 national percentile rank points on the fourth-grade reading exam, by 2.68 national percentile rank points on the fourth-grade math exam, and by 1.59 points on the seventh-grade math exam."[30] These gains are relative to the schools' own initial performance and also to the gains made over the same period by Arizona schools that did not face charter school competition.

A separate study, by Booker, Gilpatric, Gronberg, and Jansen,[31] used the rapidly growing number of charter schools in Texas to measure their effect on public school performance. By 2001–02, nearly 47,000 students were enrolled in 179 operating charter schools, up from 2,412 students in the first 16 charter schools that opened in 1996–97. Using eight-year panel data, the authors found results similar to Hoxby's for districts "facing three or four percent charter penetration."[32] This study concluded:

> Charter penetration is effective at raising performance levels of students remaining behind in traditional public schools especially when students are at schools that were performing below average in 1995–1996. Charter penetration, therefore, increases performance of students at traditional public schools, and differentially increases the performance of students at traditional public schools that were underperforming relative to other public schools.[33]

28

In North Carolina, Holmes, Desimone, and Rupp[34] found that the steady increase of charter schools from 1996–97 to 2004–05 contributed to the rise in student achievement in traditional schools. By the end of the study period, there were 99 charters. (The charter legislation allowed for 100 charters.) Their analysis controlled for student demographic variables such as race, income, and competitive proximity of charters, and they concluded that despite the meager charter school enrollment of only 1 percent of North Carolina's 1.25 million public school students,

> [c]harter school competition raised test scores in [traditional] district schools, even though the students leaving district schools for the charters tended to have above average test scores. The gain was relatively large, roughly two to five times greater than the gain from decreasing the student-faculty ratio by 1, and more than one-half of the average achievement gain of 1.7 percent in 1999–2000.[35]

Offering contrary results, Paul Teske, Mark Schneider, Jack Buckley, and Sara Clark found competitive effects on traditional public schools lacking in Springfield and Worchester, Massachusetts; Jersey City and Trenton, New Jersey; and the District of Columbia. They concluded at that time that "charter competition has not induced large changes in district-wide operations, despite the fact that a significant number of students have left district schools for charter schools."[36]

As they explained, state and district financial policies shielded traditional schools from precipitous loss of funds attributable to declining market share, and hostile competition among charter and traditional schools limited cooperation between the sectors. It seems reasonable to conclude that charter schools can confer achievement benefits on traditional schools even if they achieve only modest "market share," although traditional schools must not be protected from the financial and other effects of losing students to charter or other schools.

Knowledge and Opinion about Charter Schools

Public Views

The public knows little about charter schools, but the more people learn, the more favorable their attitudes become. A national survey of registered voters in the spring of 2005 showed that nearly two-thirds of the public said that they knew "very little" or "nothing at all" about charter schools. However, "the percent of registered voters reporting they know very little or nothing at all about charter schools is down 16 percentage points since 1999."[37]

After hearing the definition of charter schools, "those reporting that they favor them increased by 23 points (from 37 percent to 60 percent); those reporting that they oppose them increased by 13 points (from 17 percent to 30 percent); and those reporting that they don't know (or refused to answer) decreased 36 points from 46 percent to 10 percent."[38] Half of the parents in the sample reported interest in enrolling their children in a charter school after hearing the definition (or, in a small number of cases, already had a child enrolled in a charter school).

Even in a short span of two years, public opinion toward charter schools became measurably more favorable:

> Between 2000 and 2002, the Phi Delta Kappa/Gallup Poll asked Americans whether they had heard or read about charter schools. The percent of individuals saying "yes" increased to 56 percent in 2002 from 49 percent in 2000, while the percent saying "no" went down from 50 to 43 percent (and the percent answering "don't know" remained constant at 1 percent). When asked about whether they favor or oppose charter schools, those favoring increased from 42 percent in 2000 to 44 percent in 2002, while those opposing decreased from 47 percent to 43 percent (with those who don't know increasing from 11 to 13 percent).[39]

Parent Views

A survey of 300 New York City parents concluded that they are "extremely satisfied with charters in almost every aspect of schooling." Nearly half of parents in the survey (42 percent) gave their charter school an A grade overall compared with only 21 percent who gave their child's prior school an A. About half (51 percent) of parents responding said that their charter school deserves an A for quality of instruction, and 28 percent gave their charter school's instruction a B.

Nine of 10 parents reported satisfaction with charter school safety and 87 percent indicated satisfaction with parent-teacher relationships, 86 percent with the amount and quality of homework, and

85 percent with class size. Most parents (84 percent) indicated satisfaction with the school's academic quality, and similar high numbers (81 percent) were satisfied with discipline and communications from school personnel. Reenrollment is a primary indicator of a charter school's success, and, indeed, 79 percent of New York charter school parents reenrolled their children in the same charter school for the current school year, according to this study's findings.[40]

Parents with children enrolled in charter schools are satisfied, but do they accurately evaluate charter school quality? Lewis Solmon and colleagues compared the ratings of 239 charter schools by parents and experts at the Arizona Department of Education. "Across the board, state officials and parents gave nearly identical grades to the charter schools in question."[41] Parents and state educational agency staff similarly agreed on charter school ratings. The Solmon study also revealed that parents' primary reasons for choosing a charter school were "better teachers at this school" (44.8 percent), "unhappy with curriculum or teaching at prior school" (40.0 percent), and "people told me this is a better school" (34.6 percent).[42] Parents thus appear to be choosing chiefly on the basis of academic considerations and largely ignoring proximity, sports, and other nonacademic factors.

Overregulation and Underfunding

Despite their impressive accomplishments, charter schools' full potential is handicapped by lower funding than is given to traditional schools and by regulations from which charters were supposed to have been freed. Charter schools may have greater independence from state and local regulations than traditional schools, but they are still limited and heavily regulated in most of the jurisdictions in which they are allowed.

According to 2003 data from the Education Commission of the States, more than two-thirds (68 percent) of states and the District of Columbia have caps on the number of charter schools. More than half (55 percent) report that a portion of charter schools is bound by school district collective bargaining agreements with unions, and 85 percent report requirements regarding certification of charter school teachers.[43] Ironically, charter schools were originally proposed as a means of extricating schools from such stifling regulatory and contractual constraints.[44]

The *State of the Charter Movement 2005* also reveals gross inequities even considering the larger percentages of special needs and poor students in charter schools (who by federal law should be entitled to extra expenditures): "Many state charter laws provide significantly less than full funding to public charter schools."[45] Charter schools received $5,688 per pupil in operating dollars, on average, according to a national survey in 2002–03. Traditional public schools, by contrast, received $8,529, which resulted in a disparity of $2,841 per student, or 33 percent less funding for charters. Another report[46] also showed large funding disparities between charter schools and traditional public schools. In 26 of the 27 communities examined, charter schools were underfunded in amounts ranging from $1,000 to nearly $5,000 per student.

After weighting each state by its charter enrollment, the Progress Analytics Institute and Public Impact found that the "average discrepancy" was $1,801 per student, or 21.7 percent less funding for charter schools than for district public schools. Using 2002–03 data, the report categorizes four levels of funding disparity in the 16 states and District of Columbia included in the study:

> The most equitable funding for charter schools was in Minnesota and New Mexico, where there was no more than a five percent funding gap. A "moderate" funding gap (5 to 14.9 percent less for charter schools) occurred in four states (North Carolina, Florida, Michigan, and Texas) and four districts. Larger funding gaps ranged from 15 to 24.9 percent less funding for charter schools in five states (Colorado, Arizona, New York, the District of Columbia, and Illinois) and nine districts. Severe inequities of more than 25 percent between charters and district-operated schools were in six states (Missouri, Wisconsin, Georgia, Ohio, California, and South Carolina) and 13 districts.[47]

With the bulk of rigorous studies showing higher levels of achievement among charter school students, and finance studies showing that charter schools receive lower levels of per pupil funding than do traditional public schools, it is clear that charter schools are able to do more with less. They are both more effective and more efficient or productive. Charter schools, moreover, might do even better were they set free of more government regulations, as originally intended.

Conclusion

Despite the caps that states and districts have placed on their numbers and enrollment, charter schools have proliferated since their first appearance in Minnesota in 1992. Charter parents clearly prefer charter schools to traditional public schools, a preference revealed by surveys as well as long waitlists for many individual charter schools. As parents and citizens learn more about charter schools, they increasingly favor them.

Charter schools have been handicapped by receiving substantially less funding than traditional public schools and by having to comply with regulations far in excess of what was originally conceived, particularly with respect to collective bargaining with teachers' and other unions. When states and districts allow more than a small percentage of schools, say, 3 percent, to become charters, they generally have a beneficial effect on the offerings and achievement of nearby traditional schools.

The majority of rigorous studies show that charter students, on average, achieve at higher academic levels, and, more important, they learn at faster rates than traditional school students. The positive effect that charter schools have on nearby public schools is to be expected, because competition tends to bring out the best in enterprises across entire economies. The presence of charter schools compels underachieving public schools to do a better job or risk losing students and funding to the new entrants. Traditional public schools may also be induced to emulate practices that have proven successful in the charter sector.

Data on charter schools, of course, are not a true test of the idea that completely free markets in education would even more substantially and consistently increase academic achievement and parental satisfaction levels and achieve economic efficiencies that public schools cannot. Enrollment in charter schools is too small in many states and spotty in others; charter schools are still subject to heavy government regulation, and funding for charter schools lags behind that for public schools. As enrollment in charter schools grows, moreover, public school funding often goes unreduced as the public schools lose students, which means public schools are insulated from the consequences of their failure (and become even less efficient since they serve fewer students with the same amount of funding).

Still, the success of charter schools, even with these handicaps, has to be viewed as favorable to a free-market hypothesis. In the absence of domestic examples of large-scale voucher programs or true free markets in education, charter schools provide valuable and credible evidence that even small amounts of competition and choice in education have favorable results for students. Such results may arise in two ways: choice schools may simply raise achievement of their own students, and they may provide a competitive "tide that lifts all boats." As in other markets, both kinds of causation probably occur.

3. Education Voucher Effects

Education vouchers are grants to parents to cover some or all of the cost of private school tuition. These programs can be either publicly or privately funded. When funded by the state, they are simply called "vouchers" (or, occasionally, "public vouchers"). When funded by private businesses, foundations, or philanthropists, they are usually referred to as "scholarships," but sometimes the term "private vouchers" is also used.

This chapter reviews the effects of voucher programs on academic achievement for both voucher-receiving private school students and students who remain in public schools. The effects on subgroups are noted separately for African-American children and for children with learning disabilities in those cases in which they are known to differ from the aggregate effect. This chapter also assesses the impact of vouchers on school segregation and parental satisfaction. Since K–12 public voucher programs are new and small in scope in the United States, research on large-scale programs in other countries is also reviewed.

Education Vouchers in the United States

Education voucher programs vary by the number and type of students allowed to participate, the size of the voucher, and the regulations imposed on participating schools. Voucher programs can be open to all children (as in Sweden, Chile, and the Netherlands), or limited to children from low-income families (as in Cleveland, Milwaukee, and the District of Columbia), to students attending failing public schools (as in Florida's A + program and Ohio's Educational Choice Program), to students with special educational needs (as in Florida's McKay Scholarship Program and Ohio's Autism Scholarship Program), to prekindergarten children (as in Florida), or to students who live in towns that do not operate public schools at their grade levels (as in Maine and Vermont).

Table 3-1
PUBLIC VOUCHER PROGRAMS IN THE UNITED STATES,
ENROLLMENT AND NUMBER OF PARTICIPATING SCHOOLS
IN 2004–05

Program	Enrollment	Number of Schools
Cleveland Scholarship and Tutoring Program	5,675	N.A.
Florida A+ Opportunity Scholarships	763	N.A.
Florida McKay Scholarships	15,910	703
Maine Town Tuitioning Program	6,052	N.A.
Milwaukee Parental Choice Program	15,035	118
Ohio Autism Scholarship Program	270	92
Utah Carson Smith Scholarships*	138	13
Vermont Town Tuitioning Program	4,445	N.A.
Washington, DC, Opportunity Scholarships	1,733	62
Total	36,521	N.A.

SOURCE: "ABCs of School Choice, 2005–06 Edition," Milton and Rose Friedman Foundation, updated May 24, 2006.

NOTE: N.A. means not available.

*The Utah Carson Smith Scholarship Program began in 2005–06.

Unlike some other countries, the United States has no universal K–12 voucher programs currently in operation, though such a program was passed in Utah in early 2007. Most of the established programs are means tested and operate in cities where greater numbers of students and higher population densities make school choice more practical and where low-performance public schools are a well-recognized problem.

During the 2004–05 school year, public voucher programs operated in six states and the District of Columbia and enrolled approximately 36,000 students in nearly 1,000 schools or tutoring programs (see Table 3-1). Private voucher programs enrolled approximately 50,000 students in 79 programs in 2001.[1] Most private voucher programs require that applicant families be government defined as poor, and families often pay part of the tuition, typically $500 annually. Notable private programs include the San Antonio HORIZON program; the School Choice Scholarship Foundation in New York City;

Parents Advancing Choice in Education in Dayton, Ohio; the Washington Scholarship Fund in Washington, DC; and the Children's Scholarship Fund in Charlotte, North Carolina.

Controversies over Vouchers

Some proponents of education vouchers predicted that they would improve the academic achievement of students attending choice schools while also making all schools more productive and desirable. Competition, they argued, brings out the best in people and organizations, not only because it appeals to entrepreneurs who aim to profit, but also because people want to innovate, earn the esteem of others, and excel in their pursuits. Competitors provide benchmarks against which to measure individual efforts and also invaluable lessons in what and what not to do. Proponents of vouchers also argued that allowing parents to choose the schools their children attend would encourage parents to participate in their children's schooling, which, in turn, is positively related to student learning.

Opponents of vouchers predicted that there would be no improvement in the academic achievement levels of students attending schools of choice after controlling for differences in student backgrounds and the motivation of parents. Competition, they argued, is inappropriate in education and discourages and hampers good teachers and administrators seeking to work cooperatively for the good of their students. They also warned that parents may be poorly equipped to choose the best schools for their children, that minority children and children with learning disabilities would be left behind, that schools might further racially segregate, and that public schools would suffer from the loss of their best students and financial resources.

Public voucher programs often are opposed by public school boards, teachers' unions, and other public-sector unions that benefit from the status quo and fear that school choice will divert tax dollars from the budgets of traditional public schools. Vouchers receive their strongest support from African-American parents, whose children often attend the lowest-performing public schools, and increasingly by civic and business leaders who view public school underperformance as an obstacle to economic development and community improvement.

As I learned from Stanford political scientist Terry Moe, vouchers are politically controversial because they tend to split the two major political parties. Two big constituencies of the Democratic Party are African Americans and Latinos, who strongly favor vouchers, and teachers' unions and other public-sector unions that strongly oppose them. Among Republicans, advocates of the free market support vouchers because they expect competition and choice to enhance efficiency and parental satisfaction, whereas suburban Republicans may oppose vouchers because they do not want low-achieving city children enrolled in their children's schools, and they may believe they pay high property taxes for what they see as good schools in their neighborhoods.

Because of these political controversies, public voucher programs in the United States exist in only a few cities, and they are generally small in scope. Consequently, their success or failure does not constitute a conclusive test of the education market (or even the voucher idea). Certain programs, however, are sufficiently large and have been studied with sufficient rigor to shed some light on the controversies summarized above and to provide some insight into how schools and parents would react to larger-scale voucher programs. Several voucher programs in other countries, discussed below, have been far more ambitious and also reasonably well researched.

Voucher Effects on Academic Achievement

Although fewer students participate in voucher programs than attend charter schools, the random assignment of students gives researchers access to enough data to compare public and private voucher recipients to students who lost selection lotteries, which results in gold-standard randomized field trials. Eight such studies and three non-random-assignment studies have evaluated the effects of vouchers on academic achievement.

Eight Random-Assignment Studies of Academic Achievement Effects

Led by Paul Peterson, Harvard University's Program on Education Policy and Governance[2] conducted several studies of achievement by students participating for two years in private voucher programs in New York City, Washington, and Dayton. The research team found that African-American students who received scholarships outperformed African-American students who applied for but did not receive scholarships by 4 percentile points in New York, 7 percentile points in Dayton, and 9 percentile points in Washington, DC. No statistically significant effect was found for white students.

Mathematica Policy Research of Washington, DC,[3] studied the private voucher program in New York City and found a slightly stronger academic benefit to African-American students receiving scholarships (9.2 percentile points instead of 9.0) than did the Harvard study, though the effect was statistically significant only for one of the three grade levels studied. The Harvard team validly contended that the sample size for each grade level was too small to allow that conclusion to be drawn.

Researchers from Harvard, Mathematica, and the University of Wisconsin[4] studied the New York private voucher program again in 2002 and once again found that standardized reading and math test scores for African-American students who used vouchers were 9.2 percentile points higher than those of comparable African-American students who did not use vouchers. The researchers also found that, when asked to assign a grade to their children's schools, 42 percent of voucher parents gave their school an A while only 10 percent of parents not in the program gave their school an A.

Jay Greene[5] studied a private voucher program in Charlotte, North Carolina, and found that scholarship lottery winners outperformed losers by 6 percentile points after one year. A comparison of the effects on African-American versus white students was not possible because too few white students were part of the sample.

Jay Greene, Paul Peterson, and Jiangtao Du[6] studied Milwaukee's public voucher program in 1998, once again using random-assignment data, and found that lottery winners scored 6 percentile points higher on reading tests and 11 percentile points higher on math tests than did lottery losers. Cecelia Rouse[7] also analyzed data from Milwaukee's public voucher program in the same year and found that scholarship students scored 1.5 to 2.3 percentile points higher per year in math than did students in the control group.

*Three Non-Random-Assignment Studies of Academic
Achievement Effects*

Metcalf[8] studied the academic effects of Cleveland's public voucher program, though without random-assignment data and with insufficient data to adequately control for differences in student backgrounds among choice school and traditional public school families. Despite these data limitations, he found that scholarship students had "significantly higher test scores than public school students in reading and writing (45.0 versus 40.0) and science (40.0 versus 36.0). However, there were no statistically significant differences between these groups on any of the other scores.

Paul Peterson, William Howell, and Jay Greene[9] studied two schools participating in the Cleveland choice program and found that voucher students "had gains of 7.5 national percentile points in reading and 15.6 NPR in math. These gains were achieved even though the students at these two schools were among the most disadvantaged students in Cleveland." The two schools enrolled only 15 percent of all choice students and 25 percent of all voucher students who transferred from public schools.

Greene summarized the state of empirical research on voucher programs in 2001 as follows:

> There have been seven random-assignment and three non-random-assignment studies of school choice programs in the last few years. The authors of all ten studies find at least some benefits from the programs and recommend their continuation if not expansion. No study finds a significant harm to student achievement from the school choice programs.[10]

Other more recent analytic summaries of voucher evaluations come to similar conclusions.[11] This research appears to validate one of the predictions of proponents of vouchers: students attending schools of choice are likely to experience higher levels of academic achievement. Although the voucher programs studied were too small to prove or disprove predictions about the magnitude of the effects that would result from universal voucher programs, they nevertheless demonstrate that even small steps to make schools more competitive have produced measurable positive effects on student achievement.

Education Voucher Effects on Black Student Achievement

A puzzle in voucher research is that African-American students show significant achievement gains while other racial-ethnic groups do not, an important anomaly since African Americans typically lag substantially (about one standard deviation) behind whites. From his evaluations of private voucher programs in Milwaukee, Cleveland,

New York, and Washington, Harvard University's Paul Peterson concluded:

> According to the test score results, African American students from low-income families who switch from a public to a private school do considerably better after two years than students who do not receive a voucher opportunity. However, students from other ethnic backgrounds seem to learn after two years as much but no more in private schools than their public school counterparts.[12]

A RAND Corporation summary evaluation similarly concluded that "[s]mall-scale, experimental privately funded voucher programs targeted to low-income students suggest a possible (but as yet uncertain) modest achievement benefit for African-American students after one to two years in voucher schools (as compared with local public schools)."[13]

The Urban Institute summarized quantitative evaluation data on the effects of vouchers for African-American students as follows:

> The results of this research also showed that attending a private school was beneficial but only for African American students. On average African Americans who received vouchers scored .17 standard deviations higher on the combined test scores than African Americans in the control group [after one year in the program]. After two years they scored .33 standard deviations higher than their counterparts in the control group.[14]

Sustained annual gains of around .15 would eliminate the race gap in about seven years.

Two explanations for these findings seem plausible. First, African-American parents typically are more favorable toward voucher programs than are white parents. They may enter voucher programs with higher expectations than Asians, Hispanics, and whites and transfer their enthusiasm to their children and teachers.

Second, since African-American students are the largest group of students in most voucher programs, any effects on them are more likely to be statistically significant. Other things being equal, larger sample sizes are more likely to uncover effects. The smaller numbers of whites in voucher programs may make any effects for them undetectable just as a medical experiment with too few cases might not detect the effect of a superior treatment.

41

Patrick Wolf[15] studied school-level policies that could dispropor-
tionately affect African-American students in a randomized field
trial study of the Washington, DC, private voucher program. This
program, started in 1993, provides privately funded partial tuition
scholarships of up to $2,200 to families in the District of Columbia
with household income at or below 270 percent of the federal poverty
line. Scholarships can be redeemed at more than 100 participating
DC private schools. Some 1,325 elementary and secondary students
used these vouchers in the year of study, 2002.[16] Wolf's analysis
suggests that dedicated teachers, advantaged peers, and more
demanding homework assignments are likely factors that increase
academic achievement of inner-city, largely black voucher users,
rather than other factors commonly found to positively affect learning such as greater school resources, smaller school communities,
smaller class sizes, orderly and disciplined learning environments,
and a stronger sense of community.

In conclusion, the fact that African-American students benefit dis-
proportionately from education vouchers rebuts concerns that school
choice would be injurious to minorities. That white students do not
appear to benefit as much, or possibly at all, from current voucher
programs seems more likely to be due to parental motivation, but
too few whites may have been in these voucher programs to make
any benefits for them detectable.

Parents' Experiences with Vouchers

As Table 3-2 indicates, parents who have transferred their children
from public to private schools through voucher programs report far
fewer behavior and other social problems in private schools.[17]

Parents also reported substantially more school outreach from
private schools (see Table 3-3).[18]

Effects of Education Vouchers on Student Achievement in Public Schools

Education vouchers may improve the academic achievement of
students who get to attend schools of choice, but what about the
children who remain in public schools? To answer this question,
Harvard economist Caroline Hoxby compared the achievement

Table 3-2
PARENT REPORTS OF SOCIAL PROBLEMS AT PUBLIC AND PRIVATE
SCHOOLS SERVING VOUCHER PARTICIPANTS IN NEW YORK CITY,
DAYTON, AND WASHINGTON, DC

Problem	Private School %	Public School %
Fighting	32	63
Truancy	26	48
Tardiness	33	54
Cheating	26	39

SOURCE: Adapted from Paul E. Peterson, "Thorough and Efficient Private and Public Schools," in *Courting Failure,* ed. Erik A. Hanushek (Stanford, CA: Stanford Univeristy Education Next Press, 2006).

Table 3-3
PARENT REPORTS OF SCHOOL OUTREACH BY PUBLIC AND PRIVATE
SCHOOLS SERVING VOUCHER PARTICIPANTS IN NEW YORK CITY,
DAYTON, AND WASHINGTON, DC

Outreach	Private School %	Public School %
Parents receive notes from teachers	93	78
Parents receive newsletters about the school	88	68
Parents are notified when child is sent to office for first time because of disruptive behavior	93	78
Parents are informed about student progress halfway through the grading period	93	84

SOURCE: Adapted from Paul E. Peterson, "Thorough and Efficient Private and Public Schools," in *Courting Failure,* ed. Erik A. Hanushek (Stanford, CA: Stanford Univeristy Education Next Press, 2006).

gains of Milwaukee public schools facing voucher school competition with the gains of other public schools in Wisconsin that enrolled similar students but did not face competition from nearby voucher schools. She concluded:

> In every subject, achievement grew most in the schools that faced the most voucher competition, a medium amount in

the schools that faced less competition, and the least in the schools that faced no competition. . . . [The] evaluation of Milwaukee suggests that public schools made a strong push to improve achievement in the face of competition from vouchers. The schools that faced the most potential competition from vouchers raised achievement dramatically. Growth of four or more NPR points per year is highly unusual in education, yet Milwaukee schools managed such improvements in math, science, and social studies. . . . [Furthermore] the achievement effects of vouchers are likely to be understated because the control schools contain slightly more advantaged students.[19]

Low-income students in Milwaukee were first able to use vouchers in the 1990–91 school year. Since participation was initially limited to only 1 percent of Milwaukee's enrollment, many were denied admission. After eight years of dispute about the cap for the program, policymakers raised the ceiling to 15 percent (about 14,700 students) of Milwaukee's total enrollment in public schools. Poor families are eligible to apply for vouchers (but are not guaranteed to receive them) if their income is at or below 175 percent of the federal poverty level ($17,463 for a family of four in 1999–2000), an amount roughly equal to the income eligibility threshold for free and reduced-price school lunches.

A case study of Milwaukee's public schools showed that the district made program decisions that likely account for its improved academic performance. After participation in the voucher program was raised to 15 percent of public school enrollment, the public school system closed its six worst schools, developed more early childhood and full-day kindergarten programs, expanded before- and after-school programs from 1 to 82 from 1995 to 2001, and opened several new charter schools.[20]

Florida provides another setting for the study of the market effects of vouchers or even the threat of vouchers. Until a court struck it down in January 2006, the statewide A + program graded schools on an achievement scale from A to F and provided vouchers to students to use at other private or public schools if their school received two Fs in any four-year period. Four independent evaluations of Florida's program each concluded that the program improved the performance of public schools.

An early detailed analysis conducted in 2001 by Greene indicated that student achievement improved at a faster rate in schools that received an F.[21] Greene's research, using school-level achievement data, showed that academic test results were not significantly different among schools that received grades of A, B, or C. Schools that received a D, however, showed some improvement, and schools designated as failing demonstrated the greatest gains in test scores.

Greene and Winters[22] studied Florida's A+ program in 2004 and reached similar conclusions:

> The schools facing either the prospect or the reality of vouchers made substantial gains compared with the results achieved by the rest of Florida's public schools. They also made strong gains relative to those earned by schools serving similar student populations, which nonetheless avoided receiving an F.

West and Peterson[23] came to similar conclusions and also showed that the worst grades under the A+ system had greater effects than the longer-term threat of the federal No Child Left Behind Act, even though more than 75 percent of all Florida elementary schools were in "need of improvement" in 2003, most often because one or more subgroups did not make adequate yearly progress toward academic proficiency.

A fourth study, by Figlio and Rouse,[24] found public school achievement gains "consistent with the early results used by the state of Florida to claim large-scale improvements associated with the threat of voucher assignment," but noted that "much of this estimated effect may be due to other factors. . . . [T]he gains in reading scores," for example, were "explained largely by changing student characteristics." Figlio and Rouse did find small relative improvement on the high-stakes tests administered by the state but much smaller relative improvement on a lower-stakes, nationally norm-referenced test. They contended that improvements by low-performing schools "were more due to the stigma of receiving the low grade rather than the threat of vouchers," although the relative weighting seems difficult to estimate. Whatever the weighting of the psychological reasons, there is agreement about the program as a whole having a positive effect on public school performance.

Not all research has found a positive effect of vouchers on public schools. An evaluation of Washington, DC's, public voucher program after one year showed no significant effect on public school achievement.[25] The evaluators proposed several reasons: the program had no adverse effects on the traditional public school budgets, which may have reduced the incentive to respond to the competitive voucher threat; a year may have been too little time to reveal effects; and the small number of voucher students may have been insufficient to produce systemwide effects in a large city.

In conclusion, substantial evidence shows that public and private voucher programs, and the threat of publicly funded vouchers, have positive effects on public school achievement levels. Fear that vouchers would siphon away good students and needed funding is not confirmed by the limited experience to date. Competition and choice create benefits beyond those enjoyed by the students who participate directly in voucher programs.

Effects of Education Vouchers on Special Needs Students

Special needs students are categorized as having one or more physical and mental disabilities such as deafness, mental retardation, specific learning disabilities, or "behavioral disorders" (disruptive and uncontrollable behavior). In any given traditional public school, only one or a few students may be in a given category, so school staff may have difficulty providing the specialized equipment and services best for each category of students. For this reason, some states and districts have provided specialized schools for categories of students such as the blind and the partially sighted. School officials have allocated as much as four times the cost of educating a nondisabled student to special needs students' education, and some students are transported out of state for special services.

On average, special education students perform relatively poorly in school but not necessarily as poorly in adult life. Specialized schools may devote themselves to a special need such as blindness, but some parents prefer that their children be "mainstreamed," that is, placed in classes with nondisabled students—the situation they are likely to face as adults. Parents and experts differ in their views on both diagnosis and educational treatment, and the field is subject to much controversy and litigation.

Only one special needs voucher program has been evaluated, Florida's McKay Scholarship Program. Fortunately, it is large in scale and available statewide, and evaluators have compared voucher parents' opinions about their children's experiences with those of parents whose children attend nonchosen public schools.

McKay parents may choose schools that best meet their preferences for their children. This Florida program enrolls about 9,200 students with special learning needs in private schools chosen by their parents. The amount of their scholarship or voucher is equal to the tuition of the receiving school or the amount the state and district allocate to educate a student with the particular disability, whichever is lower. The scholarships range from $4,500 to $21,000 per student, with an average of $5,547.

Surveys analyzed by Greene and Forster[26] showed that more than 90 percent of McKay voucher parents were satisfied with the schools they chose, compared to one-third of parents of special needs students in nonchosen schools. Voucher parents also reported that their children endured less harassment and fewer physical attacks than did parents of similar children attending nonchosen public schools. In public schools, nearly half (46.8 percent) of the students with special needs were harassed regularly, and nearly one-fourth (24.7 percent) suffered physical assaults. Only 5.3 percent of McKay voucher parents reported that their children were being harassed on a regular basis, and only 6.0 percent reported a physical assault.

The difference in students' behavioral problems was also striking. Only 18.8 percent of parents reported that their children exhibited behavior problems in their chosen schools in the McKay program, compared to 40.3 percent of parents reporting such behavior by their children in traditional public schools.

Effects of Education Vouchers on Racial Integration

Many American public schools have historically been and still are racially segregated, with school racial concentrations often higher than 90 percent. Since the U.S. Supreme Court's 1954 ruling in *Brown v. Board of Education*, federal courts have distinguished de facto segregation attributable to housing patterns from *de jure* segregation attributable to unconstitutional government acts, usually by state and local public school boards and staff. Many states and hundreds of northern, southern, and western public school districts, particularly in large cities, remain under federal court supervision as adjudicated constitutional violators. The Dallas public school system was only recently declared unitary (i.e., in compliance with the law against dual systems).

Subsequent to *Brown*, federal courts ordered mandatory bussing to achieve racial integration. This generally meant that African-American students were bussed, sometimes long distances, to schools in white neighborhoods and, to a lesser extent, vice versa. Since parents typically wanted their children to go to neighborhood schools close to home, middle-class African Americans and whites often moved to the suburbs or enrolled their children in private schools to avoid bussing, thereby concentrating the poor in city systems. Since whites are, on average, wealthier and therefore more mobile, they moved in greater numbers, which made many urban public schools even more de facto segregated.[27]

Just as charter schools enable families to send their children to schools outside their neighborhoods, vouchers make it far easier for poor and black families to send their children to private schools, if they so choose. Jay Greene and Marcus Winters's evaluation of the first year of the Washington, DC, voucher program[28] showed that voucher students, 94 percent of whom are black, attended private schools that are more racially integrated than Washington public schools. The evaluators point out that neither public nor participating private schools in Washington are racially integrated in proportion to the city's population, but the voucher program did help create more opportunities for integration than would have otherwise existed.

Vouchers with higher dollar values offer students greater opportunity to attend less-segregated, more costly private schools. In 1999–2000, the average elementary school tuition in the United States was $3,267—$2,451 at Catholic schools, $3,503 at other religiously affiliated schools, and $7,884 at nonsectarian private schools.[29] The Washington voucher program provides up to $7,500 for students to transfer to private schools, which may contribute to its positive effects on racial segregation, compared with other programs offering smaller amounts that do not cover private school tuition and expenses.

Research on Cleveland's voucher program similarly indicates greater racial integration of voucher users. The Cleveland Scholarship Program began in the 1996–97 school year and provides up to $2,250 per student to attend 1 of 51 private schools. Greene[30] found that nearly a fifth (19 percent) of voucher students attended a racially integrated school (within 10 percent of the average proportion of minorities in metropolitan Cleveland) compared with only 5.2 percent of Cleveland public school students. Greene's research also showed "61 percent of public school students in the metropolitan area attended schools that were racially segregated (where more than 90 percent of students were of the same background) compared to 50 percent of the students attending private schools with voucher students."[31]

Religious schools were initially ineligible to participate in Milwaukee's voucher program. That prohibition was subsequently lifted, and an evaluation of the program showed that Milwaukee's voucher-accepting religious schools are better integrated than the city's public schools.[32] In 1990–91, 341 students used vouchers to attend 7 schools, and by 2001–02, 10,882 students used vouchers to attend 106 different schools.[33] While 54.4 percent of Milwaukee public school students attended racially isolated schools in 2001–02, only 41.8 percent attended similarly racially isolated private religious schools in the voucher program.[34] The program allowed some students who would otherwise have been racially isolated to attend less-segregated private religious schools. In late 2006 Gregg Forster reviewed seven valid research studies of voucher programs in Milwaukee, Cleveland, and Washington, DC, and concluded that each one showed that voucher-participating private schools were less racially segregated than public schools.[35]

Parent Satisfaction

Studies of private scholarship programs in New York; Dayton, Ohio; and Washington, DC, find high degrees of satisfaction among voucher parents. According to a comprehensive Government Accountability Office review:

> In all three cities in each year for which data are available, parents of voucher users were more likely than parents of control group students to give their child's school an "A"

on an A to F scale. These findings held true for all parents of voucher users, not only for African Americans.[36]

In all three cities, "parents of voucher users were more likely than the parents of control group students to report they were 'very satisfied' with school safety, teaching, and school curricula."[37] In all three years in New York, and in the second year in Dayton, parents of voucher users were more likely to report being very satisfied with the academic quality of their child's school than were the parents of students who did not use vouchers.

Voucher parents expressed greater satisfaction with their school's discipline, compared to parents who did not use a voucher, for all three years of the New York study and for the first year of the Dayton and Washington studies. Analysts of these results considered the estimates based on the New York study the most reliable because that study had the fewest problems with participants not returning for follow-up and families declining voucher offers.[38]

Parents who choose the schools their children attend report being satisfied with their choices, but are they making wise decisions? Survey data indicate that parents commonly choose schools for academic quality rather than other reasons such as convenience or sports opportunities. In a free society, of course, they should have the right to choose what they think is best for their children.

John Witte's analysis of America's first public voucher program showed that 88.6 percent of the Milwaukee voucher parents ranked the "educational quality in chosen school" very important. Similarly, 85.7 percent of participating parents said "teaching approach or style" was very important.[39] More than 80 percent of participants in the Milwaukee, San Antonio, and Indianapolis voucher programs said academic quality was their most important reason for choosing their children's schools.[40] The data show that parents who participate in education voucher programs are more satisfied with the results than are parents whose children must attend schools assigned to them by administrators or by their place of residence.

The research discussed so far suggests that voucher programs yield results at least as good as those of traditional public schools, that they work particularly well for African-American students, and that in no case have any categories of students fared worse under voucher programs than under the status quo. Voucher programs also benefit traditional public schools and are popular with parents, who ultimately are the consumers of educational services and, as taxpayers, are usually footing part of the bill.

Effects of Education Vouchers in Other Countries

Less research evidence is available on the modest U.S. voucher efforts than policymakers might wish to see before undertaking the major changes that extensive voucher programs would require. To gain a better understanding of the effects of large-scale programs, the next section turns to countries in Northern and Eastern Europe and Latin America where voucher programs have been operating for anywhere between one and nine decades, some on an extensive national scale.

Sweden

In 1993 the Swedish government required all local education authorities to fund schools of choice at a per student expenditure level of 85 percent of the per student cost of traditional public schools. As a result, Sweden's families did not have to pay tuition at most private schools and acquired new educational opportunities provided by schools abiding by a new open-admission policy under which schools accepted students of varying ability, ethnicity, and socioeconomic level.

Sweden formed a national agency responsible for approving new independent schools. Swedish students are able to chose any public or participating private school, including those governed and operated by for-profit firms. This newly created nationwide educational marketplace—though limited by price controls, an official curriculum, and other government regulations—led to increased competitiveness, improved student achievement, and greater parental satisfaction with children's schools.[41]

New voucher schools were established in a broad cross section of neighborhoods, including high-income areas as well as locales serving predominately working-class and immigrant populations. In terms of scale, the number of independent schools saw a fivefold increase, and private-sector student enrollment increased fourfold. Contrary to anticipated fears, neither economic segregation nor isolation of special needs students materialized.

Netherlands

The Dutch voucher system began in 1917, and the private education sector now enrolls 76 percent of all primary and secondary students.[42] Religious foundations (Catholic, Protestant, Jewish, and Muslim) run most private schools, though some are nondenominational schools or schools with special pedagogical approaches. State funding covers capital costs, and the local municipality covers operating expenses for private voucher schools. The Netherlands does not allow voucher-accepting private schools to be operated for profit.

Government regulations hold schools accountable to a standard curriculum, a certain number of teaching hours, information reporting, and assessment methods. Belfield and Levin report, "Evaluations of the education system in the Netherlands show positive reports both for freedom of choice and academic effectiveness, and without any dramatic inequities or apparent loss in social cohesion."[43] Parents report high satisfaction in finding schools to meet their children's needs, and the Netherlands performs well in international test score comparisons. Catholic schools in the Netherlands demonstrate better academic gains than do public schools, and yet religious differences among schools do not incite social divisiveness.[44]

Czech Republic

The Czech Republic introduced voucher programs after the fall of communism, which spurred the creation of private schools in areas of pent-up demand and poor-quality government-run schools. In the 1990s the Czech Republic expanded educational choice by funding private schools with a "two-part tariff," that is, 50 percent of the total support for a state school is automatically given to a private school, and state officials determine an additional amount such that total funding does not exceed 90 percent of what is received by a state school. Given this small disparity between public funding levels for private and public schools, private schools introduced additional fees for supplemental education services, which may limit access to low-income students with greater educational needs.

According to Belfield and Levin: "Even as the number of private schools grew from zero to over 440 within a decade, the absorption of students into these schools was correspondingly high: most private schools are smaller than public schools."[45] Since the new school choice policies increased options in low-income areas, which tend to have the worst-performing schools, low-income families have the widest range of choice and benefit from increased privatization in the Czech Republic.

Chile

In 1982 Chile introduced a universal voucher program that decentralized education governance to local municipalities.[46] Enrollment-driven subsidies were given to public and private schools that elected to participate. All students could choose to enroll at either type of school. Under this policy, private school enrollments increased as both religious and independent for-profit private schools proliferated.

Some early test score comparisons showed that students attending for-profit voucher schools performed similarly to students in public schools, while Catholic school students performed slightly better. Students in elite private schools that did not participate in the voucher program scored the highest in test score comparisons.[47] The students, however, may have been different from one another in ways not considered by these early studies, which makes their results questionable.

Claudio Sapelli found in later research that, after controlling for budget differences and for socioeconomic characteristics of students and their peers, students in private subsidized (that is, voucher) schools outperformed those in public schools.[48] Sapelli, moreover, pointed out that public schools that saw an exodus of students to the private sector are not closed; rather, they receive extra funding from municipal governments to ensure that teachers' salaries can still be paid. This extra funding was not offered to private schools. Hence, he explains: "[P]ublic schools do not have to choose between supplying an education that attracts enough students to allow the school to pay its wage bill and laying off staff. The choice those schools actually face is whether public school teachers are to be paid to teach large or small classes."[49] Subsidized public schools also received extra funding to educate poorer students, which put private schools at a competitive disadvantage in their efforts to serve such students.

53

As Andrew Coulson has pointed out, test score analyses by Francisco Gallego show that both public and private voucher schools have been closing the gap with elite nonvoucher private schools.[50] Market forces, in other words, may be the tide that indeed lifts all boats—and this result was achieved even though unsubsidized Chilean private schools could set their own admissions policies, just as such schools can in the United States.

Colombia

Beginning in 1991, more than 125,000 students in Colombia received vouchers covering about half the cost of private schooling. The Programa de Ampliacion de Cobertura de la Education Secundaria offers families residing in low-income communities with children in the public schools the option of using a voucher at a nonprofit school.

In a randomized field experiment, evaluators found that vouchers considerably increased the probability of a student receiving a private school scholarship (though only half of the private schools accepted vouchers).[51] Voucher recipients remained in school for a slightly longer length of time, and fewer of them repeated a grade, as a result of choosing a school that met their satisfaction. Three years after the program began, and controlling for other factors, voucher students scored higher than other students, the equivalent of attaining an extra year of schooling.[52]

Conclusion

Considering the research reviewed in this chapter as a whole, it may be concluded that public and private education vouchers almost certainly have positive effects on academic achievement by students attending both chosen and nonchosen schools. Claims that vouchers would disadvantage poor and minority children or children with special educational needs, or lead to greater segregation, are unsupported by the research on existing voucher programs.

Studies show that voucher parents choose schools mainly for academic reasons and that they are generally much more satisfied with their schools' services than are public school parents. Parents also report that voucher schools are safer, more secure environments for their children. Voucher programs in the United States may be too small to provide definitive evidence that universal vouchers would produce the positive outcomes predicted by advocates, but large-scale foreign voucher programs demonstrate considerable success despite the extensive government regulation to which they are subjected.

Appendix: Features of Voucher Programs in Various Nations

A growing body of international research on school voucher programs uncovers significant gains in parent satisfaction, student achievement, and school diversity. With dramatic increases in governmental funding for private schools, families benefit from the widening selection of schools and indicate greater satisfaction with the schools they choose. Student achievement is at least as good, and usually better, in private voucher schools. This research literature also indicates that universal voucher programs do not create social divisiveness. With public funding for schools of choice regardless of family income, student performance increases overall (see Table 3-A1).

Table 3-A1
FEATURES OF VOUCHER PROGRAMS

Nation	Year Initiated	Unique Funding Features	Target Approach/ Population Affected	Summary of Results
Sweden	1993	All local governments fund schools of choice at 85% of the per student cost of traditional public schools. Swedish citizens choose any government-run or privately run school for their children. The majority of private tuition cost at most for-profit schools is subsidized by government, regardless of family income. No restrictions on religious schools' eligibility for vouchers.	Of the Swedish population of approximately nine million, 6 percent of children of compulsory school age and 10 percent of upper secondary school children attend independent schools. More than half of independent schools owned by limited liability companies.	Increased overall student achievement. Improved parent satisfaction. Fivefold increase in the number of students in independent schools.

| Netherlands | 1917 | State funding covers capital costs, and local municipality covers operating expenses for private, nonprofit voucher schools. For-profit schools cannot receive voucher payments. Religious foundations run most private schools. For both state-run and private voucher schools, government regulates the curriculum, the number of hours worked by teachers, information reporting standards, and testing. | Private education sector now enrolls 76% of primary and secondary students, which is more than 2.26 million students. The estimated population of children in the Netherlands aged 0–14 years in July 2005 was 18.1% of total population (male: 1,523,316; female: 1,453,232). | High parent satisfaction. Strong international student achievement performance. Catholic school students outperform public school students (despite lower average socioeconomic status). Reduced some tensions over what should be taught among Christians and between Christians and secularists. |

(continued)

Continued

Nation	Year Initiated	Unique Funding Features	Target Approach/ Population Affected	Summary of Results
Czech Republic	1990s	"Two-part tariff," i.e., 50% of total support for state-run schools automatically given to private schools, and state officials give additional discretionary amount, totaling up to 90% of funding for state-run schools. Private schools charge additional fees for supplemental education services to make up the difference.	The 2006 population estimate for the Czech Republic is 10,265,231.	Most private schools are smaller than public schools. Growth of private schools was substantial. Public funding of private schools widened school choice, particularly for low-income students.

| Chile | 1982 | Schools receive monthly payments based on the number of students enrolled. Vouchers are also paid to students. Monetary rewards provided to high-achieving schools. Voucher amounts do not vary by family income. Public schools receive additional funding for lower-income students that private voucher schools do not receive, creating a disincentive for low-income families to choose private schools. | Universal voucher program available to all students. The estimated population in April 2006 of Chilean students aged 0–14 years: 24.7% (male: 2,035,278; female: 1,944,754). | Private school enrollment increased. Religious and secular for-profit private schools proliferated. Catholic school students outperform others slightly. Both public and private voucher students have been catching up with students in elite private tuition schools. |

(continued)

Continued

Nation	Year Initiated	Unique Funding Features	Target Approach/ Population Affected	Summary of Results
Colombia	1991	Low-income families can use vouchers to send children to nonprofit private schools.	Only half of private schools accept vouchers. Voucher recipients typically remained in school for a slightly longer period of time. Over 125,000 received vouchers covering about half the cost of private schooling in 1991. The total population of Colombia is 41,800,000 (2005 estimate); children aged 0–14 years are 30.3% of the total (male: 6,683,079; female: 6,528,563), 2006 estimate.	Voucher recipients increased their probability of receiving private school scholarships to attend private schools. Increased satisfaction with their schools reduced number of students repeating grades. Three years after admission, voucher students had higher test scores than other students.

SOURCES: David Salisbury and James Tooley, eds., *What America Can Learn from School Choice in Other Countries* (Washington: Cato Institute, 2005); and Clive R. Belfield and Henry M. Levin, *Education Privatization: Causes, Consequences, and Planning Implications* (Paris: UNESCO/International Institute for Educational Planning, 2002).

4. Private School Effects

Private schools in the United States and in other countries offer another opportunity to measure the effects of school choice. Before the spread of charter schools and voucher programs, comparisons of public and private schools were the most common source of data invoked in debates about school choice. Such comparisons are still instructive. While controlling for parental motivation and other confounding factors is challenging, the number of students attending private schools around the country is typically much larger than the number of students attending charter schools or participating in voucher programs, and students usually remain enrolled for longer periods, which allows any effects to become more clear. Parent-funded private schools are also less regulated than charter schools and schools participating in voucher programs, which allows for a sharper comparison of chosen and unchosen schools.

This chapter reviews research on the effects of private schools on academic achievement, efficiency, racial integration, parental satisfaction, and civic engagement by students. Also included is a review of international data, which can be revealing because the share of students in private schools and the possibility of measuring choice effects are often greater in other countries than in the United States.

Private Schools in the United States

For two centuries, private schools were the dominant form of American K–12 schooling. From the founding of the first colonies through the middle of the 19th century, most schools, many of them with only one room for all grades, were privately owned, privately managed, and funded by tuition and government subsidies from tiny units of local government.[1] Curricula, instruction, and tests emphasized English literacy, mathematics, history, and science. Most historians agree that by 1840 the northern states had the highest literacy rate in the world—about 90 percent—unlike today's poor showing of the United States among industrialized countries, described in Chapter 1.[2]

Table 4-1
PRIVATE SCHOOL ENROLLMENT IN THE UNITED STATES IN 2004

School Characteristic	Number (in thousands)	Percentage
Roman Catholic	2,365	46.2
Other religious	1,836	35.8
Independent	922	18.0
Total	5,123	100.0

SOURCE: National Center for Education Statistics, *The Condition of Education 2006*, pp. 112, 134, http://nces.ed.gov/programs/coe/2006/pdf/04_2006.pdf.

Despite such early success, local governments around 1850 began placing restrictions on private schools, reducing aid to them, and founding government-owned and government-operated schools. Prominent advocates of government schooling, including Horace Mann in Massachusetts and Henry Barnard in Connecticut, successfully argued for tuition-free government-operated schools for all children. Compulsory school attendance laws were introduced in 1852, and by 1918 all states had passed laws requiring children to attend at least elementary school.

Catholics and other religious groups opposed what they saw as Protestant favoritism in government schools and created their own private sectarian schools. In 1925 the U.S. Supreme Court ruled in *Pierce v. Society of Sisters* that states could not compel children to attend public schools, ensuring a continued place for sectarian schools in the United States.

Today, private schools account for about 11 percent of total K–12 enrollment in the United States. Nearly half of all private schools are Catholic (see Table 4-1). About a third are operated by other religious groups, and the remainder are secular (that is, independent of religious groups).

Although the performance of private schools provides some insight into what an extensive school choice program might look like, today's private schools operate in a distorted marketplace that often reduces real competition. As economist John Wenders writes:

> [P]rivate schools have been forced into a niche market that operates under the inferior quality umbrella held up by the public schools. While private schools must be more market

oriented, and leaner, than their public counterparts, they are also protected in their niches by the inferior quality public school umbrella under which they serve. Faced with a clumsy, bureaucratic monopolist as a competitor, the private schools may not be anywhere near as efficient as their reliance on parental choice would suggest.[3]

Thus, if private schools themselves were subject to greater competition, they might be expected to respond with substantially greater effectiveness, efficiency, and consumer satisfaction. Were sizable numbers for-profit, they might be expected to respond more quickly and more fully, and such schools might further be expected to stimulate other schools to improve substantially.

Private Schools and Elite University Attendance

If competition and choice work well in education, and if the absence of the profit motive does not excessively undermine their benefits, then students attending private schools ought to have higher achievement levels than similarly prepared students attending government schools. Achievement comparisons have been a source of controversy since the seminal and provocative 1981 study of Catholic schools by James Coleman.[4] Like his successors, Coleman investigated Catholic schools because they are numerous and relatively homogeneous. Before turning to this research, consider the general comparison of public and private schools.

The data clearly show that students attending private schools score higher on standardized tests and graduate and enter college at higher rates than students attending public schools.[5] For example, private schools have outstanding records for their graduates gaining admission to elite public and private universities. A 2006 survey[6] of elite public and private college and university admissions offices reveals that in 2005, on average, 41 percent of the freshman enrollees attended private K–12 schools (see Table 4-2). Since the enrollment in private schools in the United States is only about 11 percent of all U.S. K–12 students, private school students are four times as likely as public school students to gain admission to elite private colleges and universities. Even if private schools did not yield superior achievement and achievement gains, it seems likely that many parents would like to have their children exposed to peer groups bound for such prestigious institutions.

Table 4-2
ENROLLMENTS OF PRIVATE HIGH SCHOOL STUDENTS IN
ELITE COLLEGES AND UNIVERSITIES

College or University	Percent of Private School Students among Enrolled Freshmen
Amherst College	40
Bowdoin College	46
Brown University	42
Cornell University	23
Dartmouth College	38
Duke University	37
Georgetown University	49
Middlebury College	48
Massachusetts Institute of Technology	22
Pomona College	35
Princeton University	40
Stanford University	30
Swarthmore College	35
University of California, Berkeley	86
University of Chicago	33
University of Pennsylvania	48
Yale University	46
Average	41

SOURCE: "Enrollments of Private High School Students in Elite Colleges and Universities," *Wall Street Journal,* September 15, 2006, p. W10.

Private vs. Public School Achievement

But do these effects of private schools remain after controlling for family income, parents' level of education, and other possible confounding factors? Researchers seeking answers face major obstacles. The private school sector is small and relatively heterogeneous compared to the public sector. Private schools vary greatly by size, spending level, curriculum, and student demographics, which makes it less likely that studies will yield clear, consistent results. Private and public schools in different states also use different achievement examinations, which adds to the difficulty of making comparisons. In addition, differences in family motivation and background rather than school effectiveness may cause achievement differences between the two sectors.

All of these methodological difficulties were apparent in a study released in 2006 by the U.S. Department of Education purporting to show no positive effect of private schools on academic achievement.[7] In an extensive critique,[8] Paul Peterson and Elena Llaudet pointed out the study's fallacious drawing of causal inferences from single-point-in-time achievement scores; the underestimation of the prevalence of disadvantages such as poverty, limited English proficiency, and special needs in private schools; and the overestimation of these characteristics in public schools. The study also incorrectly controlled for differences in student absenteeism and the availability of books and computers in the home, which are factors that vary by school sector. These incorrect controls further biased its results.

After fixing such flaws, Peterson and Llaudet found that Catholic, Lutheran, Evangelical Protestant, and independent school fourth- and eighth-grade students all scored higher on National Assessment of Educational Progress tests in mathematics and in reading than did their public school counterparts after appropriate statistical controls were used. Peterson and Llaudet, however, were careful to avoid any firm causal inferences from single-point-in-time achievement scores from small samples.

An earlier study by John Chubb and Terry Moe,[9] using a national data sample, found that private secondary school students learned more than those in public schools, after controlling for socioeconomic status and other possible confounders. They attributed the effect of private schools primarily to greater "school autonomy," a subject addressed below.

The most comprehensive comparison of public and private school achievement shows that private schools excelled at the two grade levels tested in mathematics, reading, science, and writing in the National Assessment of Educational Progress. The differences were larger in all subjects in eighth than in fourth grade, which apparently shows the private school advantage grows with additional years of schooling.[10] As indicated in Table 4-3, minority students achieved more in private schools than their corresponding groups did in public schools. Students in private schools whose parents had not completed high school had the greatest gains, although private

Table 4-3
PRIVATE SCHOOL PERFORMANCE ADVANTAGE FOR FOUR ETHNIC
GROUPS AND PARENTS' HIGHEST LEVELS OF EDUCATION

Ethnic Group	Private School Advantage in Achievement Score Points
Hispanic	10
Black	5
White	5
Asian	4
Parent education	
Less than high school	18
Graduated from high school	15
Some education after high school	11
Graduated from college	16

SOURCE: Adapted from Paul E. Peterson, "Thorough and Efficient Private and Public Schools" in *Courting Failure*, ed. Erik A. Hanushek (Stanford, CA: Stanford University Education Next Press, 2006), p. 221.

school students at all levels of parent education outscored their public school counterparts.

Catholic vs. Public School Achievement

Because Catholic schools are much more numerous and relatively more homogeneous than other groups of sectarian and independent private schools, several rigorous studies have contrasted them with public schools. James Coleman and Thomas Hoffer, for example, responded to criticism of their earlier work by analyzing student gains and taking student socioeconomic status into better account.[11] They again found a significant and positive effect of Catholic schools.

More recently, Anthony Bryk, Valerie Lee, and Paul Holland employed state-of-the-art research methods on achievement gains data and found that Catholic schools significantly outpaced public schools.[12] From a detailed analysis of longer-term effects, Derek Neal concluded that Catholic schooling significantly increased high school and college graduation rates and later wages among urban minorities; it offered modest gains to urban whites and had a "negligible" effect on suburban students.[13]

In a review of many studies, Patrick McEwan[14] concluded that Catholic elementary schools have modest positive effects on poor minority students in grades 2–5 and mixed effects on other students and grades. But, "[i]n contrast, the evidence on attainment is strikingly consistent, indicating that Catholic schools increase the probability of high school completion and college attendance, particularly for minorities in urban areas." Eide, Goldhaber, and Showalter[15] extended this conclusion by showing that Catholic school students were more likely to attend selective colleges than were public school students.

The Character of Private Schools

Numerous investigators have observed private schools, and sometimes contrasted them with nearby public schools, to discover why they are more effective and efficient and have greater appeal to parents. As early as the 1970s, Thomas Sowell[16] reported case studies of schools located in Atlanta, Baltimore, New Orleans, and Washington, DC, that educated a long list of black graduates who made outstanding breakthroughs, including a state superintendent of schools, a Supreme Court justice, and a military general. Sowell attributed the success of these schools to strong principals and a social order concentrated on achievement and discipline:

> "Respect" was the word most used by those interviewed to describe the attitudes of students and parents toward these schools. "The teacher was *always* right" was a phrase that was used again and again to describe the attitude of the black parents of a generation or more ago.... Even today, in those few instances where schools have the confidence of black parents, a wise student maintains a discrete silence at home about his difficulties with teachers, and hopes that the teachers do the same.[17]

Chubb and Moe's detailed and paradigm-shifting 1990 study identified several characteristics of "effective schools" and then found that school sector—public or private—was by far the most significant factor in determining whether a school was effectively organized. A private school principal, for example, is less likely to face interference in school management by central authorities such as boards and superintendents. The resulting autonomy enables principals to adopt "clear academic goals, strong educational leadership, professionalized teaching, ambitious academic programs, team-like organizations—these effective school characteristics are promoted much more successfully by market control than by direct democratic control."[18]

On the basis of extensive observations of Catholic schools, Valerie Lee[19] concluded that Catholic schools do well because they offer a delimited core curriculum followed by all students, regardless of their family background, academic preparation, or future educational plans; engender a strong sense of community exemplified by frequent opportunities for face-to-face interactions and shared experiences among adults and students at school events such as athletics, drama, and music; and expect teachers to see their responsibilities beyond classroom subject matter and extending into hallways, school grounds, neighborhoods, and homes. Lee also noted that Catholic schools are decentralized; funds are raised and decisions are made largely at the school level.

Paul Peterson and I studied the organizational features, achievement, and cost differences between all Catholic and public schools in three New York City boroughs (Brooklyn, Manhattan, and the Bronx).[20] We found that student achievement in Catholic schools exceeded achievement of students in public schools with comparable low, medium, and high levels of poverty. High-poverty Catholic schools did particularly well compared to high-poverty public schools and made substantial progress in closing achievement gaps.

When comparing costs, we first subtracted from public school budgets all of the expenditures for government-funded programs for poor students and those with limited English and special needs. We also subtracted the extra public school costs of transportation, food services, and central office and community board staff that oversee schools. Even after these adjustments, Catholic schools' costs per student were only 46.8 percent those of public schools.[21]

Corroborating a Chubb-Moe finding about private schools, my interviews and observations in Catholic schools revealed fewer centrally determined policies. The schools had strong site-level leadership, demanding and largely academic curricula followed by all students, frequent communication with parents, and higher student retention based on parental and student satisfaction.

The public school staff I interviewed operated in a very different environment. Central office and community boards and staff, following U.S. Department of Education and New York state rules and regulations, played major roles in instituting, funding, regulating, and ordering school-level policies and practices. In local schools, high staff turnover undermined curricula, instruction, and disciplinary policies. Central office administrators changed schools' attendance boundaries and even grade levels without consulting parents or school staff. In several hundred classrooms, I frequently saw teachers unable to keep students attentive, books being sparsely used, and many students who had not completed assignments. Children often held off-topic conversations, rested or slept at their desks, and walked around and in and out of their classrooms.

The level of courtesy, respect, and fairness observed in Catholic schools was much higher. Disciplined teaching and learning were pervasive. The principals maintained a clear focus on academic programs and sustained engaged leadership. In general, decisions related to instruction and the school sites were made at the school site rather than mandated from above. On the whole, classes received academically challenging tasks and completed them. My observations in Catholic schools showed students keeping notebooks of assignments, completing homework and subject-related notes, and receiving daily grades.

Though these observational studies concern samples of private African-American and Catholic schools, Chubb and Moe's analysis explains why similar findings are likely when Jewish, Lutheran, Muslim, and other sectarian and nonsectarian private schools are examined.

In summary, private schools exhibit superior academic achievement levels even after controlling for family socioeconomic status and other factors, though whether such factors can be completely controlled for is a subject of continuing controversy. The reason private schools excel is the way they are organized—strong principals with clear academic visions, the freedom to adopt and pursue policies, etc.—and this organizational form in turn is both made possible and strongly encouraged by market competition, producer autonomy, and consumer choice.

Effects of Private Schools on Efficiency

A large scholarly literature compares public and private provision of many services.[22] John Hilke's survey[23] of more than 100 independent studies of privatization (moving from public to private provision of a service) showed cost reductions of between 20 percent and 50 percent, even though the quality of services and customer satisfaction were just as high or higher. Private firms, in other words, are up to twice as efficient as government agencies at delivering goods and services.

Proponents of school choice have said that private schools have similar efficiency advantages over public schools and that school choice programs would produce substantial savings for taxpayers or enable higher-quality private schooling to be purchased with current levels of spending. Comparisons of public and private per student spending offer a partial test of this claim. Such comparisons are difficult, however, because public school expenditures are variously calculated in different localities and states, and private school tuition may be subsidized just as some parents and firms privately contribute, though perhaps to a lesser extent, to public schools.

Several studies take such factors into account and still show greater efficiency of private schools. Andrew Coulson's study of Arizona schools, for example, showed that private schools spend about 66 percent of the amount spent by public schools.[24] John Wenders[25] compiled similar estimates of private school per pupil spending as a fraction of public school costs. The estimates he reports for several types of schools—Catholic schools with and without parish subsidies, nonsectarian, all private, and all private without Catholic and Lutheran schools—cluster around 55 percent.

For those who want to look at *taxpayer* rather than total costs, it is reasonable to compare private school tuition with public school expenditures. Table 4-4 compares per pupil spending by public schools with average private school tuition for six cities and the national average.[26] Unfortunately, separate figures for public elementary and secondary (or high) schools were unavailable. However, even though secondary schools are substantially more costly than elementary schools, private *secondary* schools cost 31 percent less than the average for *all* public schools. Private school tuition in all cities sampled (except the special case of Washington) and the United States as a whole is substantially lower than public school spending.

For an overall estimate of public and private school costs, if we assume that enrollment is constant across grades and that private schools are divided into grades 1–8 and 9–12, the weighted estimate of tuition at all private schools is $5,140, which is 42 percent less than public school per student spending, amounting to a difference

Table 4-4
PUBLIC SPENDING AND PRIVATE TUITION IN SIX LARGE AND
MIDSIZED CITIES AND THE UNITED STATES FOR THE
2002–03 SCHOOL YEAR

City	Public School per Student Spending	Median Private Elementary School Tuition	Median Private Secondary School Tuition
New Orleans	$ 5,797	$2,386	$3,895
Charleston, SC	$ 6,701	$3,153	$4,057
Houston	$ 7,089	$4,325	$6,150
Philadelphia	$ 8,303	$2,504	$4,310
Denver	$ 9,919	$3,528	$5,995
Washington, DC	$11,009	$4,500	$6,920
United States	$ 8,830	$4,689	$6,052

SOURCES: David F. Salisbury, "What Does a Voucher Buy? A Closer Look at the Cost of Private Schools," Cato Policy Analysis no. 486, August 28, 2003, http://www.cato.org/pubs/pas/pa486.pdf; and National Center for Education Statistics, *Digest of Education Statistics, 2002*, Table 61, http://nces.ed.gov/pubs2003/2003060b.pdf.

NOTE: The authors sampled big city school systems in several parts of the country for which data were available. For the special case of Washington, where foreign diplomats, congressional people, and well-heeled lobbyists reside, more realistic estimates of median tuition were obtained for neighboring Maryland and Virginia counties; they accord well with the other comparisons.

of $3,690 based on the figures in Table 4-4. Multiplying this difference by the number of public school students (54.5 million in 2005) yields $201 billion, the hypothetical and roughly estimated savings if all public school students joined those in private schools (assuming no subsequent rise in average tuition attributable to that shift).

Since private schools cost so much less than public schools, allowing parents to choose private schools for their children should in principle allow huge taxpayer savings while leaving per pupil spending by public schools unchanged. To estimate these savings, David Salisbury[27] compiled analyses of available costs of school choice programs in Arizona, Cleveland, Florida, Maine, Pennsylvania, and Vermont and for proposed plans for Baltimore, New Hampshire, South Carolina, Utah, and Vermont. Of course, estimating such savings requires assumptions about enrollment trends and public spending decisions that would have occurred in the absence of the choice programs, which make calculations questionable.[28]

Even so, such estimates with reasonable assumptions nearly always point to large savings for taxpayers. For example, Milwaukee's public schools estimate that they would have to spend $70 million more a year on operations and up to $70 million on capital projects if the Milwaukee School Choice program were to end.[29] A taxpayer organization in Florida estimates that the Florida Corporate Income Tax for Scholarships Program will save the state $1 billion over eight years.[30] Pennsylvania's Education Improvement Tax Credit is estimated to have saved the state's taxpayers between $147 million and $205 million.[31]

In conclusion, the assertion that private schools are more efficient than public schools is amply documented in the literature. Private schools, on average, spend thousands of dollars less per pupil than do public schools. Since private schools achieve at least as much as public schools and probably more, they are obviously more efficient economically. Expanding school choice programs to enable more parents to choose private schools should save taxpayers large amounts of money, or enable more educational services to be purchased without exceeding current spending levels.

Effects of Private Schools on Tolerance, Civic Participation, and Social Integration

Even if private schools are more efficient, they might still be criticized for being homogeneous enclaves of intolerance, un-Americanism, or even tribalism. Such criticism ignores the traditional American right to congregate and the lessons of the first two American centuries, a period when private education was prevalent and private schools helped assimilate millions of immigrants into the American economy and society. Still, it is an empirical question whether or not private schools foster intolerance and civic indifference.

To answer this question, David Campbell[32] analyzed a large national data set on secondary school students that contains several questions on tolerance for anti-religious activities. Perhaps surprisingly, he found that Catholic school and nonsectarian private school students were more likely to be tolerant than were public school students. These students were also more likely than public school students to participate in civic activities such as volunteering, public speaking, and writing editorial letters on public issues.

Private, alternative, and magnet schools apparently have stronger civic climates, which, in turn, may lead to increasing political participation and voting behavior later in life. Daniel McFarland and Carlos Starmanns studied student councils in hundreds of high schools across the country and examined the written constitutions of 207 public and 66 private high schools. They found:

> Alternative schools—charter, magnet, or private—seem to offer opportunities for meaningful political participation greater than even the wealthiest public schools. Student councils typically consist of 20 to 40 officers, regardless of school size, so these generally smaller schools enable a greater percentage of students to hold office. And because alternative schools tend to have a clear mission, their constitutions try to uphold school values—by encouraging the election of moral exemplars, for example.[33]

Another way to examine the question is to compare the attitudes of college students educated in private and public schools. Wolf, Greene, Kleitz, and Thalhammar[34] surveyed 1,212 students in introductory American government courses at the University of Texas–Austin, the University of North Texas, the University of Houston, and Texas Christian University. Their survey results indicate that the privately educated students have substantially higher tolerance scores than do those educated in public high schools.

Schools with the strongest civic climates tend to increase civic participation in later life. Campbell[35] analyzed Youth Studies Series data obtained in interviews with high school seniors, their classmates, and parents in 1965 and from the same students interviewed again in 1973 and 1982. Campbell found that "cohesive schools," including those with a homogeneous political composition, foster higher rates of voting in later adult life.

But are privately educated ethnic minorities more tolerant, particularly those with large fractions of recent immigrants? To answer this question, Greene, Giammo, and Mellow[36] analyzed data from the Latino National Political Survey, a national sample of adult Latinos. Those educated predominately in private schools were significantly more likely to be tolerant than were those who had been educated in U.S. public and foreign schools. For example, Latinos who received their education entirely in private schools were willing to tolerate the political activities of their least-liked group substantially more frequently than those who never attended private school (holding all other factors statistically constant). Privately educated Latinos, moreover, were more likely to vote and more likely to join civic organizations.

These appear to be the most rigorous studies available, and they show a consistent pattern favoring private schools' capacity for developing valued social attitudes. The findings certainly contradict the stereotype of private schools as enclaves of intolerance. Yet, because of parental attitudes and other difficult-to-measure conditions, there is a possibility that private school students might have developed more valued attitudes had they gone to public schools. So, the research is not quite conclusive.

Effects of Private Schools on Racial Integration

Several empirical studies have found that the parents who are the most likely to choose their children's schools tend to be somewhat more likely to be white and of higher socioeconomic status than nonchoosers. It does not follow, however, that private schools are segregated or would become segregated under a universal school choice program.[37] As Greene[38] points out, rather than blame parental bigotry, it is reasonable to think that wealthier parents simply can afford to do what the majority of parents, rich and poor, say they would prefer to do if cost were not an obstacle—send their children to private schools. For this reason, students from white and wealthier families are somewhat overrepresented in private schools. In addition, Italians, Irish, Poles, and other groups are most often white and tend to send their children to Catholic schools for religious rather than racial reasons.

Because they are often appealing and distinctive, private schools may allow and encourage voluntary integration. To investigate this view, Jay Greene examined the racial composition of a random sample of public and private school students' classrooms, collected by the National Education Longitudinal Study. He found that "private school students were significantly more likely to be in classrooms whose racial composition resembled the national proportion of minority students and significantly less likely to be in classrooms that almost entirely consisted of white or minority students."[39] Greene's analyses showed that private school students are more likely to report greater levels of cross-racial friendship and fewer instances of racial fighting than are public school students.[40] He also found that voluntary choice in public school systems diversified racial composition:

> Public schools with more students from outside their attendance zones, that is with more magnet program or transfer students, had higher rates of integration. It appears that choice systems, where schooling is detached from housing, are better able to transcend racial segregation in housing patterns. Traditional public schools, however, appear to replicate and perhaps reinforce racial segregation in housing.[41]

Research on Milwaukee and Cleveland, which have voucher programs, shows that students choosing their schools were more likely to attend schools that were racially representative of the broader community. They were less likely to attend racially homogeneous schools than were traditional public school students.[42]

Private Schools in Other Countries

Private schools in other countries provide an additional database for research on the effects of private schools on academic achievement. Andrew Coulson[43] analyzed statistically controlled studies carried out in India, Pakistan, Indonesia, the Philippines, Thailand, Vietnam, Tanzania, the Dominican Republic, Chile, and the United States. As shown in the Table 4-5, the results showed an overwhelming advantage of private schools. Of 50 comparisons that could be found for six criteria, 41 (82 percent) showed a private-sector advantage.

Similarly, James Tooley and Pauline Dixon compared outcomes and costs in the two sectors in low-income countries including Ghana, India, Kenya, and Nigeria.[44] Their summary indicates that

75

Table 4-5
NUMBER OF FINDINGS ON PRIVATE- AND
PUBLIC-SECTOR ADVANTAGE

Criterion	Private Advantage	No Significant Difference	Public Advantage
Achievement	20	5	2
Cost efficiency	10	—	1
Parental satisfaction	4	—	—
Order/discipline	3	—	—
Graduates' earnings	2	1	—
Condition of facilities	2	—	—
Total	41	6	3

SOURCE: Andrew J. Coulson, "How Markets Affect Quality: Testing a Theory of Market Education against the International Evidence," in *Educational Freedom and Urban America*, ed. David Salisbury and Casey Lartigue Jr. (Washington: Cato Institute, 2004).

achievement test scores of the poorest students in these poor countries were considerably higher in private than in government schools at between half and a quarter of the teacher salary costs. They find great success taking place in private schools, often contrary to the assumptions of educational authorities and foreign experts.

Priyanka Anand, Alejandra Mizala, and Andrea Repetto's analysis of the Chilean school voucher program, which included nationally standardized controls for parent socioeconomic status, community demographics, per student spending, and other possible influences on achievement, showed significant private-public school differences favoring private schools, and also strongly suggested that the achievement of students that moved from public to private schools was significantly and positively affected.[45]

Conclusion

The effects of private schools in the United States on academic achievement, costs, racial integration, tolerance, and active citizenship have been studied by many researchers over many years. Higher admissions to elite colleges, exposure to people of different backgrounds, and later civic community involvement are all hallmarks of a private education.

Little of the evidence, however, attains the "gold standard" of random assignment of students to schools, and it is compromised somewhat by the difficulty in controlling for parental socioeconomic status, parent and student motivation, and other factors. The largest and most rigorous U.S. studies, however, repeatedly find positive effects of private schools, and they are corroborated by studies in foreign countries, which are often larger and more rigorous than the U.S. research.

5. Geopolitical Area Choice Effects

The three preceding chapters focused on the effects of charter schools, education vouchers, and private schools on students who attend schools of choice as well as those who remain in traditional public schools. In all three cases, positive effects on both categories of students were cited.

Market effects may also be assessed by measuring the relative degree of school choice and competition within geopolitical areas such as parts of cities, cities, counties, states, and nations and comparing the educational outcomes across areas with varying degrees of choice. In principle, market pressures are higher when public and private school choice programs combine to expose themselves and traditional public schools to real competition, when school districts are small enough to cause interdistrict competition for students and taxpayers, when public school organizations are small and decentralized, and when public schools rely on local rather than state funding sources (thereby forcing them to compete with other districts to attract and retain residents).

Since choice and competition vary considerably from place to place, research on their effects is often more robust than studies of charter or voucher schools, which tend to be few in number and new or only a few years old. However, choice concentration research usually relies on statistical (regression) analysis to control for confounding factors, and so it does not achieve the "gold standard" of random-assignment studies. Large-scale studies in the United States and elsewhere nevertheless provide creditable evidence of "market effects," particularly when combined with the generally accepted conclusion that market competition among providers benefits consumers.

Literature Reviews

Two comprehensive reviews of the literature on choice concentration effects have been conducted. The first, reported in 2001 by political scientists Paul Teske and Mark Schneider,[1] included about 25 large-scale, rigorous, quantitative studies and about 75 qualitative case studies of schools in the United States. The authors examined a variety of outcomes. They explained:

> A combination of evidence is important in a domain in which economists, political scientists, sociologists, educational scholars, and others often read work only in their own disciplines. Moreover, while other researchers have reviewed various pieces of the choice literature, most are focused on only one aspect or type of choice. Here a broader analysis is sought.[2]

Teske and Schneider found a research consensus that "parents are more satisfied with choice, that they report using academic preferences to make choices, and that they tend to be more involved with their child's education as a consequence of choice."[3] Referring to public and private choice programs generally, they conclude,

> While not all of these studies conclude that choice enhances [academic] performance, it is significant to note that the best ones do, and that [we] did not find any study that documents significantly lower performance in choice schools.[4]

Also reported in 2001, the second literature review, by economists Clive Belfield and Henry Levin,[5] examined more than 40 studies of school competition. The studies reported analyses of the effects of the percentages of students enrolled in private schools and decentralized public school systems (where competition is engendered by a greater number of smaller school districts within a county or state). They concluded:

> A sizable majority of these studies report beneficial effects of competition across all outcomes, with many reporting statistically significant coefficients. Those outcomes included test scores, graduation rates, teacher salaries, housing prices, and adult wages.[6]

The many U.S. studies reviewed by Teske and Schneider, and Belfield and Levin, usually concerned school choice in single states and metropolitan areas. Two recent and much larger studies, described below, corroborate these literature reviews. The first concerns the effects of choice in 39 countries; the second looks at an index of choice in all 50 states.

Competition in 39 Countries

Ludger Woessmann, a research associate at the Kiel Institute of World Economics in Kiel, Germany, combined data from the United Nations Educational, Scientific, and Cultural Organization (UNESCO) and the World Bank on public spending per student in secondary education, from the Organization for Economic Cooperation and Development (OECD) on institutional features such as the distribution of decisionmaking powers in public school systems and enrollment in private schools, and student-level academic achievement data from the Third International Mathematics and Science Study (the largest international student achievement survey ever conducted) to create a representative sample of about 250,000 students from a population of more than 30 million students in 39 economically advanced and emerging economies.[7]

Woessmann found that competition from private schools and the degree of centralization of authority in public school systems varied dramatically among countries, providing considerable natural variation for measuring the effects of competition on achievement. His analysis showed that, for all the countries, increased per student spending "does not generally raise educational performance," and, in particular, there is "no systematic relationship between resources and performance across time within most countries in the OECD [30 economically advanced countries of the 39 included in the study]."[8]

Higher levels of private school governance, however, were associated with higher academic performance:

> Students in countries with larger shares of their enrollment in privately managed schools scored significantly higher in both math and science. If the share of enrollment in privately managed schools was 10 percentage points higher, students scored 6 points better in math, 5 in science. The effect was even larger when only those private institutions that were financially independent were considered.[9]

As was pointed out in Chapter 4, several OECD countries have attained considerable recent success with publicly financed voucher or scholarship programs that enable students to attend privately managed schools. (In these cases, public funds go not directly to schools as in the case of charter schools but to families that can use the voucher at schools they choose.)

Competition in the 50 States

Jay Greene[10] developed an Education Freedom Index (EFI) to measure the amount of school choice present in all 50 states. As revised in 2002, the index is an equally weighted average of five measures of educational options:

- the availability of charter school options,
- the availability of government-assisted private school options (e.g., vouchers),
- the ease with which one can homeschool one's child,
- the ease with which one can choose a different public school district by relocating, and
- the ease with which one can send a child to a different public school district without changing residence.

According to the EFI, the greatest amount of school choice can be found in Arizona, which has the largest number of charter schools in the nation, imposes few regulations on homeschoolers, has a tax credit program for private school tuition, and encourages interdistrict public school choice. With only one school board for the entire state, few charter schools, and heavily regulated homeschooling, Hawaii has the least amount of educational freedom.

Using statistical (regression) analysis, Greene isolated the choice effect from the significant and potentially confounding effects of median household income and the percentage of ethnic minorities in each state, and two insignificant variables (average class size and per student expenditures). He found that the EFI scale was significantly associated with test scores. A one-point increase on the EFI scale (which ranged from .84 to 2.94) was associated with a 24-point increase on the Scholastic Aptitude Test and a 5.5 percent increase in the number of students performing proficiently on the National Assessment of Educational Progress (NAEP). By comparison, a $1,000 boost in median household income corresponds to only a .3 percent increase in the percentage of students performing proficiently on the NAEP exam. Thus, both aptitude and achievement were substantially associated with school choice.[11]

Andrew Coulson developed a more comprehensive index of educational market freedom in 2006, which weighs both the extent of parental choice and both public and private schools' autonomy over such things as curriculum, testing, budgets, staffing, and teacher certification. A controlled statistical (regression) analysis taking into consideration demographic factors showed that the index explained more of the variation in a combined measure of test scores and graduation rates "than did race, wealth, presence of nuclear families, or parental education," which are well-known to be related to achievement.[12]

Competition among School Districts

In a 1956 article titled "A Pure Theory of Local Expenditures,"[13] economist Charles Tiebout pointed out that government jurisdictions such as counties and school districts compete with one another to attract and retain citizens. Communities provide a diversity of offerings, and rational citizens choose to move to or stay in those that best satisfy their weighting of perceived benefits, including such things as cultural amenities, well-regarded schools, rurality, proximity to work and recreation, and low taxes.

Competition among communities for residents can foster competition, efficiency, and the matching of freely chosen interests with public offerings in a manner resembling private markets. Tiebout's article led to many empirical studies of the demand for public amenities such as public libraries, policing, sanitation, and health services. The "Tiebout effect," as it has come to be called, explains a wide variety of local government phenomena such as why urban and regional governments use zoning laws to prevent "free riding" by citizens who want to build small homes in communities with high property wealth and low tax rates and why big, inefficient cities lose residents.

The Tiebout effect can also explain why some public schools are better than others.[14] In 1992 I first became interested in the possible benefits of small districts and local funding, and so I carried out the first study to compare school district size and reliance on state rather than local spending and student achievement.[15] The study used a random sample of students within the 37 states and the District of Columbia that participated in the National Assessment of Educational Progress academic testing program. I found that student achievement was inversely proportional to average school district size (after controlling for state demographics). The smaller the share of K–12 expenditures paid for by local districts, moreover, the worse the achievement. As many studies have shown, per student expenditures had no relation to achievement.

Other researchers have studied school district size and achievement and come to similar conclusions. Melvin Borland and Roy Howsen[16] may have been the first to employ the Herfindahl Index to measure the effects of Tiebout choice in public school districts. The Herfindahl Index is a measure of industry concentration that can range from zero (fully competitive) to one (fully monopolistic and consisting of a single provider).[17] The Federal Trade Commission defines industrial markets below 0.1 as unconcentrated, between 0.1 and 0.18 as moderately concentrated, and above 0.18 as concentrated.[18] By these standards, education markets are highly concentrated, that is, substantially uncompetitive.[19] Borland and Howsen's research on Kentucky school districts concluded that school districts with a Herfindahl Index of more than 0.50 had significantly lower achievement scores than districts with scores of less than 0.50.

Caroline Hoxby analyzed data from the National Education Longitudinal Study, which contained a greater number and range of metropolitan and district sizes than those in Kentucky.[20] She found large effects of interdistrict competition: with a 1 percent increase in the Herfindahl Index of interdistrict choice, available 8th-grade reading scores, 10th-grade math scores, and 12th-grade reading scores increased between 3 and 6 percentile points.[21]

In 2005 Jay Greene and Marcus Winters[22] conducted a similar state-level analysis. They also found a substantial and significant negative effect of district size on graduation rates and no effect of per student expenditures. They concluded that lack of competition in states with generally large districts—Florida, Hawaii, and Nevada—reduces student attainment.

For more than a half century, policymakers have unfortunately increased the size of school districts, often in a fruitless attempt to achieve "economies of scale."[23] In the 1937–38 school year, the total number of traditional public school districts was about 119,000. The number of districts dwindled to fewer than 15,000 by 2001–02.[24] The result, as the research clearly shows, has been less competition between school districts, which is associated with lower levels of student achievement.

Some states still continue to pursue the counterproductive consolidation of small school districts into larger ones. For example, Arkansas recently consolidated its 308 school districts into 254 larger ones. Other states, such as Illinois and Arizona, have recently considered consolidating school districts that they consider particularly small. Several studies indicate, if anything, that breaking up the largest districts such as Los Angeles would be a wiser policy.[25]

Decentralized Montana exemplifies the positive results achieved with a small state funding ratio and a large number of tiny school districts.[26] Montana's student achievement results have consistently ranked at or near the top of U.S. state achievement rankings, and its school districts have as few as a few hundred students.[27] In a state with mostly small school districts, the school board members, administrators, and teachers often personally know students, their siblings, and their parents. The parents and other citizens also tend to know one another and their elected board members, and it is worthwhile for them to talk with each other about school problems. It is rational for them to inform themselves about school issues since their votes count heavily in school board elections. None of this tends to be true of large school districts.

Organization Size and Bureaucracy

As the number of school districts has fallen, the number of students per district has risen by a factor of more than 10, from 214 to 2,683.[28] Schools and school systems became larger, and a few gigantic big-city school districts came to enroll several times more students than the number of *citizens* in some western states. There are good reasons to suppose, and data to confirm, that larger and more bureaucratic school districts are less productive because of inefficiencies and dysfunction that would not exist in a marketplace composed of smaller competing institutions.

The optimal size of an organization depends on the ends to be achieved. Large organizations, particularly manufacturing firms, may become efficient by searching for the single best choice and reducing unit costs by large-scale manufacturing, purchasing, or sale ("economies of scale"). Larger size, however, makes it more likely that organizations will have internal and external communication problems that make it difficult to satisfy customers and to achieve the organization's nominal mission. Those problems can be solved, but not without cost.

Research by psychologists and sociologists shows that organizations as diverse as business firms and psychiatric units of hospitals face difficult problems in achieving their stated ends when they grow large.[29] Consider the plight of the large airlines and automobile manufacturers. Their problems may be viewed as psychological impediments to information flow and deterrents to economic efficiency allowed by limited market competition (typically under government-protected monopolistic or oligopolistic conditions). In the terminology of organizational psychology, the "coordination costs" of communicating among departments and administrative levels divert money, time, and attention from the organizations' ultimate purposes. "Agency problems" mean that nominal governance is remote from service delivery and customer satisfaction, allowing each level of administration to mistakenly report to or misunderstand information from levels above and below it. Sometimes such errors may be deliberate to enhance the power and compensation of members of parts of the organization. To control coordination and agency problems, big organizations must impose complex rules, but setting forth and following these rules divert further resources and discourage efficient innovations and sensitivity to customer preferences.[30]

When businesses grow so large that solving coordination and agency problems becomes too expensive, the "creative destruction" of competitive markets forces firms to return to their optimal size or go out of business. If their boards and senior staff don't reform themselves, the firms are acquired by or merged with other firms, or they go bankrupt. Monopolistic government-run organizations that have grown too large, however, may continue to operate and grow indefinitely since they remain undisciplined by market competition. Traditional public schools and school districts are classic cases since their dissatisfied parents have had little recourse except moving or paying tuition to private schools.

Government budgets are usually arcane, and few citizens take the trouble to master them. School district control is often "captured" by special interest groups, particularly teachers' unions.[31] Their members are far fewer in number than voters, taxpayers, and their client students and their families, but their members are typically far better informed about their organizations and have agreed-upon, narrow self-interests. They are strategically organized and able to exert strong influence over often less well informed boards, administrators, legislators, governors, mayors, and other civic leaders. The rewards for each union member and public school administrator in salary and working conditions are large, but the costs may be imperceptible to taxpayers, except in the aggregate, since increases in school costs may be a minute fraction of total taxes.

With respect to K–12 education, larger units of government such as states and large city and metropolitan districts are likely to be led by people who are less well informed about the needs and preferences of smaller communities within their purview. It seems unlikely, for example, that Chicago school board members could even name the several hundred schools they are responsible for overseeing, let alone get to know and represent the preferences and concerns of individual parents. Special interests may find it easier and more efficient, moreover, to influence policy when decisionmakers are fewer in number and located in a single place. Concentrating on a state legislature, for example, would seem to be easier and more efficient than trying to influence thousands of local school board members nominally overseeing several hundred school districts in the typical state.[32]

About one-third of the K–12 students are enrolled in fewer than 2 percent of the school districts.[33] With as many as 1.1 million students in 1,203 schools and average school sizes just short of 1,000 in New York City, the biggest city school systems are well-known for high costs and poor performance. They illustrate the problems of extreme centralization; complex departmentalization; intermediate governing units leading to inefficient, uncompetitive schools; and withdrawal of middle-class children from big city schools to private schools and the suburbs.

The shortcomings of New York City's public schools were described in the last chapter, and Chicago public schools further illustrate these big-city problems. Only about 54 percent of Chicago public school students actually graduate.[34] According to the 2005 Trial Urban District Assessment, administered as part of the National Assessment of Educational Progress,[35] only 14 percent of Chicago's fourth graders and 17 percent of Chicago's eighth graders are reading at or above proficiency. An astounding 40 percent of fourth graders read below even "basic" levels—scoring so low as to literally be "off the charts." Only 13 percent of fourth graders have math skills considered at or above proficient levels, and only 11 percent of eighth graders have this skill level.

The enormous size, bureaucracies, and inefficiencies of big-city schools in the United States help explain why teachers constitute approximately half of all school district staff in the United States in contrast to between 60 and 80 percent of school staffing in Europe.[36] School districts in Texas devote approximately 59 cents of every dollar spent on education to classroom instruction, California about 54 cents, and Illinois only 46 cents.[37] Private schools, as reported in the previous chapter, devote much higher percentages of their budgets to classrooms and less to administration.

State versus Local Funding

Another factor influencing the amount of competition and choice in a school system is how heavily schools rely on state rather than local governments for their funding. Near the bottom of state achievement are California and Hawaii states that rely most heavily on state rather than local taxes. Public schools that can rely on state funding don't have to compete with schools in other districts for local taxpayers willing to support them. They lose the incentive to operate effectively and efficiently and to be accountable to local parents and business owners.

Unfortunately, states have paid a growing share of K–12 funding in the United States. Because of litigation, they are increasingly compelled to provide equal per pupil funding to local schools. An unintended consequence of this policy is that parents who care the most about providing a quality education for their children tend to send their children to private schools at higher rates than they otherwise would, which gives them less reason to support neighborhood public schools by participating as accountable board members and engaged parents, volunteers, or boosters.

Local funding gives local property owners a rational interest in the quality of public schools, even if they have no children in school, because good schools enhance real estate values. As realtors often stress, homeowners in districts with effective and efficient schools are rewarded with high, rising property values. A literature review by Yinger, Bloom, Borch-Supan, and Ladd found that 27 of 28 studies confirmed this local expenditure "capitalization effect."[38]

Caroline Hoxby[39] compared the performance of schools in New Hampshire, where the state's share of school funding was just 7.0 percent in 1996, to that of six comparison states (Massachusetts, California, Hawaii, Connecticut, Indiana, and Washington), where schools rely more heavily on state funding. She found that public support for public schools, measured by per pupil spending, rose more slowly in four of the six control states than it did in New Hampshire from 1980 to 1990. Enrollment in private schools during that period fell 11 percent in New Hampshire—evidence of satisfaction with public schools—but rose in five of the six control states and fell by only 2 percent in the sixth state (Massachusetts).

Hoxby found that New Hampshire beat every control state in change in college graduation rate, beat five states and tied with one on student earnings, and reduced the percentage of students who are unemployed more than five states but less than one. Overall, New Hampshire's locally funded schools were clearly providing superior service and, in return, enjoyed greater public support than schools in states that increased their reliance on state aid.

Conclusion

A review of 40 U.S. studies shows positive effects of choice and competition within geopolitical areas. The largest international study of schools ever made, moreover, showed that the greater the degree of school choice in 39 countries, the higher the achievement test scores. Two large-scale studies of the degree of choice in the 50 states came to the same conclusion.

Choice effects are most apparent when charter, voucher, or private schools compete head to head with traditional public schools in achievement, graduation rates, and other outcomes. But choice also has systematic and constructive effects even when they occur in subtler and less direct ways, such as the benefits of smaller districts and those that rely more heavily on local than on state funding sources. Citizens in such districts rationally involve themselves more deeply in school affairs and reap beneficial consequences.

6. Customer Satisfaction

As documented in the previous chapters, school choice generally improves achievement and several other outcomes that parents, citizens, and legislators think are socially valuable and individually beneficial. But one measure of success may be more important than all others: does school choice satisfy parents and students, the most direct beneficiaries or "customers" of schooling? And what are the views of the public?

This chapter explains why customer satisfaction should matter and reveals how satisfied parents and students are with the educational status quo, school choice generally, and charter and voucher schools in particular. The views of parents, students, and the public at large are contrasted with those of teachers and school administrators to understand how they diverge and why this divergence has important implications for public policy.

When choosing a restaurant, people care for more than the objective measures of calories, nutrients, and costs alone; they also care about subjective taste, décor, and ambiance—matters of personal preference. In the case of school choice, interview and questionnaire surveys are essential for assessing opinions of the various interested parties. Surveys are, of course, widely used in market research to measure attitudes toward products and services and in politics to estimate the voter appeal of candidates and policies. Nonprofit and for-profit organizations employ surveys to find out how people view them and how they might best improve their goods and services. What do surveys reveal about citizens', parents', and educators' views about schools and school choice, and why should these views matter?

Why Parental Satisfaction Matters

When choosing a doctor, people may make decisions based on a combination of objective and subjective factors. Perhaps they should take note of their candidates' medical school, special training and other qualifications, reputation among peers, claims of malpractice, prices charged, personal demeanor, and other information. But few people actually collect and systematically weigh such evidence.

People often choose their doctor seemingly at random or on the recommendations of acquaintances, and they may decide to return to that doctor on the basis of the experience of the initial encounter. They may consider whether or not the doctor seemed to listen to them, sympathize, and understand their concerns. They may ask, Did the doctor seem insightful, professional, and experienced? Did the treatment prescribed seem to work?

As seemingly unscientific and subjective as this decision appears, and despite the possibly life-and-death consequences, Americans generally choose their doctors and change them when they wish. Similarly, parents choose charter, voucher, or private schools for their children. Seldom is there a single objective criterion for determining the best decision.

Parents in the United States can properly assert their right, recognized by long tradition and law, to direct the education of their children.[1] Some legal experts place the right of parents to control the schooling of their children at the foundation of all other civil liberties.[2] Indeed, the U.S. Supreme Court ruled in *Pierce v. Society of Sisters* (1925) that

> [t]he fundamental theory of liberty upon which all governments in this Union repose excludes any general power of the state to standardize its children by forcing them to accept instruction from public teachers only. The child is not the mere creature of the state; those who nurture him and direct his destiny have the right, coupled with the high duty, to recognize and prepare him for additional obligations.[3]

In *Zelman v. Simmons-Harris* (2002), moreover, the U.S. Supreme Court upheld Cleveland's school voucher program, with the majority writing, "[I]n keeping with an unbroken line of decisions rejecting challenges to similar programs, we hold that the program does not offend the Establishment Clause."[4] Thus, vouchers can be used for parochial school tuition as long as the decision is the parents'.

It is doubtful that an "expert" can do a better job of choosing a school for a child than can a well-informed parent.[5] In their book *Education by Choice: The Case for Family Control*, Coons and Sugarman write that the current system of assigning most students to public schools is based on the notion that "local government agents make better school assignments for individual children they have never met than would the family, even were the family to be supported by professional counseling."[6] They also point out that "the question is not whether the judgment of the isolated and unassisted family is superior to the professional cadre of a school or a district. It is rather, when all available knowledge, personal and professional, about the particular school is assembled, to whom shall society commit the final choice."[7]

When parents are allowed to choose, survey research summarized by Andrew Coulson[8] shows that parents place a high value on academic achievement. "Topping the list of responses in all polls of independent-school parents is academic quality," he reports. For example, the U.S. Department of Education–sponsored National Household Survey in 1993 showed that parents who chose independent schools for their children most frequently named a "better academic environment" as the primary consideration in their choice.[9]

Parents are also likely to choose wisely. In 2001 Caroline Hoxby reported comparisons of parents' ratings of their child's public school with the school's value-added achievement (defined as the difference between a student's 10th- and 8th-grade scores in reading and math). She found that only 15 percent of parents were "highly satisfied" with their schools if they were in the lowest quartile of gains, showing that parents were aware and upset that their children's schools were academically failing. Some 44 percent of parents with children in schools in the highest quartile reported being "highly satisfied."[10]

Parents may not always make the right choices. As Milton and Rose Friedman write: "No doubt, some parents lack interest in their children's schooling or the capacity and desire to choose wisely. However, they are in a small minority. In any event, our present system unfortunately does little to help their children."[11]

Parents' School Choice Preferences

Survey research shows that large numbers of parents would prefer to choose their children's schools. One recent national survey showed that 57 percent of parents with children now attending public schools would send them to private schools if vouchers were available.[12] Only about 1 in 10 parents can afford private schools because public funds go almost exclusively to traditional public schools.

According to a Public Agenda survey,[13] the majority of parents of public school students would choose private schools if tuition were not a concern. That survey found that 55 percent of all parents and 67 percent of inner-city parents would choose private schools. Even higher percentages of African-American families support school choice. According to survey research by the Harwood Group, some 80 percent would choose private schools if they could afford the tuition.[14]

These numbers may seem at odds with the findings of the professional educators' society, Phi Delta Kappa. In 2006 PDK reported apparent declines in public support for choice, with only 36 percent of the public describing themselves as "favorable" toward education vouchers, while 60 percent were opposed.[15] As Terry Moe first pointed out, the reason for the discrepancy lies in PDK's change in the question wording. The latest version of PDK's survey asks, "Do you favor or oppose allowing students and parents to choose a private school to attend at public expense?" As Terry Moe concluded:

> PDK's "at public expense" item does not even come close to meeting these basic criteria [of maintaining the same question from year to year and in stating the purpose of vouchers]. The central purpose of a voucher program is to expand the choices available to all qualifying parents, especially those who now have kids in public schools. But the PDK item does absolutely nothing to convey this information. It says nothing about choice, nothing about public school parents' being eligible to participate. Instead, it focuses entirely on private school parents and asks respondents whether the government ought to be subsidizing them. Vouchers are presented, in effect, as a special-interest program for an exclusive group.[16]

Moe's data, taken from other national surveys with less-loaded questions, indicate 56 percent support for vouchers in 2000 and 62 percent in 2001. In fact, in 2001 a more neutrally worded PDK question read, "Would you vote for or against a system giving parents the option of using government-funded school vouchers to pay for tuition at the public, private, or religious schools of their choice? Sixty-two percent of respondents expressed support.

In 2004 and again in 2005, Harris Interactive conducted polls using the "loaded" PDK language and a more neutrally phrased question: "Do you favor or oppose allowing students and parents to choose any school, public or private, to attend using public funds?" In 2005, 60 percent of respondents were favorable and only 33 percent were opposed.[17]

Because of stronger inner-city and minority preferences for private schools, it seems likely that the demands for choice will continue to grow. The U.S. Department of Education's *Condition of Education 2005* shows that students from nonwhite backgrounds grew from 22 percent to 42 percent from 1972 to 2003. The demographic projections indicate that minority students will eventually be the majority in U.S. schools. Thus, since minorities that prefer choice will become majorities, the vast majority of parents are likely to prefer a choice of which school their children attend.

In sum, the majority of the public favors publicly funded vouchers, and the percentages appear to be growing. Private schools, there seems little doubt, best meet the standard of consumer satisfaction. These findings are corroborated by the previously discussed over-subscription to public and private voucher programs and the need for choosing students by lottery at private and charter schools.

Public Dissatisfaction with Traditional Public Schools

Surveys also reveal that the public is increasingly aware of the poor standing of American schools, the lack of achievement progress, and the threat to individual and national welfare of ineffective, inefficient K–12 education. For example, polling by Hart and Winston in 2005 found that only 9 percent of adults agree that schools set high expectations and significantly challenge most high school students.[18] A 2005 survey by Peter D. Hart Research Associates found that only 24 percent of recent high school graduates said that they faced high expectations and were significantly challenged.[19]

The 2006 PDK public opinion poll showed that 32 percent of respondents gave public schools a C, 9 percent a D, and 5 percent an F. This means that nearly half (46 percent) of the respondents thought the schools were average or worse. PDK nevertheless celebrated the results as showing: "There has been no decline in public support for public schools. Approval ratings remain high and remarkably stable."[20] It's difficult to imagine a private firm being content with such customer views.

The 2002–03 National Household Education Survey, conducted by the National Center for Education Statistics, found that only 57 percent of parents with children attending traditional public schools were "very satisfied."[21] In contrast, 68 percent with children attending public schools of choice, 75 percent with children attending secular private schools, and 78 percent with children attending religious private schools were "very satisfied."

Terry Moe summarized the results of public opinion surveys[22] and concluded that the public believes the public school system

- is outperformed by schools in the private sector;
- is inequitable, particularly on class grounds;
- adopts undesirable means of promoting diversity;
- is too intolerant of religion;
- gives parents too little influence;
- has schools that are too large; and
- should make better use of market-like mechanisms.

Sizable numbers of "customers" of public schools are clearly unhappy with the current public schools. Unfortunately, most parents have little choice but to allow others to determine what schools their children attend, even when it is well-known that the local public schools are failing academically.

Satisfaction with Charter Schools

The public is much more pleased with charter schools than it is with traditional public schools, although many do not understand them. A 2006 survey by the Glover Park Group[23] found that only 57 percent knew the meaning of charter schools. However, after hearing them defined ("independent public schools that are free to be more innovative and are held accountable for improved student achievement"), 74 percent favored expanding them, and 62 percent favored lifting state legislative caps that curtail their growth. Common elements of charter schools were even more strongly favored by voters:

- 85 percent favored giving parents more options for where to send their child to school;
- 83 percent favored giving schools more flexibility to design curriculum; and

- 90 percent favored holding students, teachers, and parents accountable for improving student achievement.

Of parents with school-aged children, 55 percent said they would be interested in enrolling their child in a charter school.

Homeschooling as an Indicator of Opinion

In 2003 parents and others educated at home some 1.1 million youngsters who would otherwise be age-eligible for K–12 schools.[24] Comparable to the size of the charter school sector, homeschooling had grown to 2.2 from 1.7 percent of the K–12 age-eligible population in 1999.

Many homeschoolers belong to the religious right, but others are on the countercultural left or are simply unhappy with the poor standards, the violence, and dominant peer culture of traditional schools. Various surveys of homeschooled students suggest that they outscore from 75 to more than 90 percent of traditional public school students and that they suffer no more college or adult psychological adjustment problems than do traditional school students.[25]

For five years I served as a judge for an independent charitable organization that awarded strictly merit-based scholarships to high school students, mostly applying to Ivy League and other elite universities, who had perfect or near perfect scores on the Scholastic Aptitude Test for college admission, had passed advanced college level courses while in high school, and had shown other evidence of advanced studies such as winning state and national academic competitions. At a celebration dinner for Midwestern students, I sat with seven recipients. At the table were two homeschooled students, one of whom was a young woman who was representing the United States in the International Mathematics Olympiad, which pits against each other the very best secondary school mathematicians in each of several dozen countries. This anecdote is hardly definitive, but it helped me to shed my doubts about homeschooled people.

Available data do not allow us to draw a causal relationship between homeschooling and advanced academic achievement, but the growth of homeschooling certainly demonstrates a high level of discontent with traditional public education. Homeschoolers are willing to give up a "free" public service that often costs $7,000, $15,000, or even more per year to deliver. Homeschooling often requires one adult to stay home to teach one or more children, a sacrifice that should be measured in lost earned income as well as reduced career potential.

Homeschooling can be expected to continue to increase in popularity thanks to the use of innovative technology by charter schools and homeschoolers. Luis Huerta, Maria-Fernanda González, and Chad d'Entremont report that an estimated 60 Internet-based charter schools are online in 15 states and currently enroll 16,000 students, which is about 10 percent of national charter enrollment. An additional 52,000 students are enrolled in homeschool charters allowed in California and Alaska.[26]

If they lack expertise in advanced or specialized subjects such as calculus or Greek, charter managers and homeschoolers can turn to the 27 online Internet courses provided by the College Board, which has long offered advanced placement examinations to high schoolers for college credit. The extraordinary growth of broadband Internet services, technology-based education in universities and firms, and discontent with traditional schools is promoting K–12 innovations, especially in choice schools and among homeschoolers.[27]

Public Educators' Opinions

Opinion surveys show a large gap between the views of educators and those of their customers, parents and students. Educators, for example, tend to oppose individual accountability, educational standards, and testing. On the other hand, a Public Agenda national survey of high school students showed that three-fourths believe that stiffer examinations and graduation requirements would make students pay more attention to their studies.[28]

In another survey, three-fourths of high school students said that schools should promote only students who master the material. Almost two-thirds reported that they could do much better in school if they tried. Nearly 80 percent said students would learn more if schools made sure they were on time and did their homework. More than 70 percent said schools should require after-school classes for those earning Ds and Fs.[29]

Leaders of traditional public schools differ sharply from their customers. A national Public Trust survey showed that 76 percent of superintendents and 59 percent of principals report that "students graduating from middle school have learned the reading, writing, and math skills they will need to succeed in high school," but only

Table 6-1
Perceived Degree of Academic Challenge in Schools

Statement	Principals	Teachers	Students
The teachers have high expectations of students	56%	39%	25%
This school has high academic standards	71	60	38
The classes are challenging	67	48	23

Source: Harris Interactive, "The MetLife Survey of the American Teacher 2001: Key Elements of Quality Schools," http://www.metlife.com/WPSAssets/26575530001018400549V1F2001ats.pdf.

33 percent of high school teachers agree. Similar percentages of district and school leaders report that "a high school diploma means a student has learned the basic academic skills of reading, writing, and math." Yet only 54 percent of high school teachers agree.[30]

Table 6-1 reveals how elementary and secondary school educators and students differ in their perceptions of the rigor of their schools' academic programs.[31]

Former dean of the Harvard Graduate School of Education Theodore Sizer portrays the charade of challenging standards in *Horace's Compromise,* which describes the common pattern of a teacher who gains orderly and easygoing relations with his students by telling them the absurdly easy questions he will ask on a test. He gains the approval and admiration of his principal even though his and his students' efforts are at a pathetic minimum.[32]

The preference for achieving easygoing relations and high student self-esteem through low standards is documented in Tom Loveless's 2006 Brookings Institution Report.[33] Even though they think their schools are unchallenging and even though they rank poorly on international mathematics achievement surveys, far greater percentages of American students expressed higher confidence in their mathematics skills than did their peers in Korea and Japan who usually top the achievement surveys.

The apparent slackness of many practicing educators may derive from views prevalent in the schools of education they attended. A 1997 Public Agenda survey of education professors[34] showed that 64 percent thought schools should avoid competition. More favored giving grades for team efforts than favored grading individual accomplishments. Only 12 percent thought it essential for teachers to expect students to be neat, on time, and polite, compared to 88 percent of the public. Only about a fifth of the professors agreed with the public that they should insist on correct spelling, grammar, and punctuation from their students. Only 37 percent thought it essential for teachers to learn how to maintain an orderly classroom.

The difference in views between educators and their customers helps explain why the 2001 federal No Child Left Behind Act, strongly supported by both Democrats and Republicans, has nevertheless faced massive resistance from educators and is at risk of failure or outright repeal. One of NCLB's objects was to pressure repeatedly failing public schools to reform or make choice available to families.

The NCLB sets out a series of remedies that must be implemented when schools' performance is deemed unsatisfactory. At various stages, districts must notify parents that their children's school is failing; provide money and opportunities for parents to have competitive private tutoring; and, in the end, "restructure" the school by closing it, replacing its staff, or commissioning private groups to manage it. Three years after the passage of NCLB, more than 1 in 10 public schools already faced sanctions for failing to make adequate yearly progress (AYP) in achievement for at least two continuous years, and some risked immediate sanctions since failing to make AYP even once.[35]

As William Howell pointed out,[36] however, public school districts severely limit choice. They block parents of students in failing schools from choosing private tutoring or sending their children to successful public or private schools. Educators lack any incentive to let parents know their rights. For example, few Massachusetts parents eligible to transfer their children to successful schools were actually informed that their children's current schools were failing.

According to Paul Peterson: "Although 69 percent of parents attending schools in ten urban districts in Massachusetts say they have heard of NCLB, and 52 percent said they know about its choice provisions, only 24 percent said they had obtained their information from the school district.[37] The news media, not the school district as required by law, were the most important source of information."[38] As other surveys discussed above have shown, many of these parents would have been likely to enroll their children in private schools, especially had they been clearly informed of the failure of their children's present school.

Conclusion

Parental satisfaction is an important measure of the success of schools. Parents have the right and duty to guide and oversee their children's education, have the strongest incentives to do it well, and have shown the ability to choose wisely. Largely aligned with parents' views, students say they prefer greater academic challenges and accountability from their schools. The public increasingly wants parents to be able to choose the schools their children attend, whether public or private. And when allowed to choose charter, voucher, or independent or sectarian private schools, parents are more satisfied. Also indicative of discontent with schools is the estimated one million U.S. children being homeschooled.

On these points, public educators' views differ generally and sharply from those of their parent, student, and citizen clients. They generally maintain that their curriculum offerings are sufficiently rigorous, and they adamantly oppose school choice. Their long-standing views appear to explain the continuation of poor results even with substantially rising expenditures. Such prevailing views may continue to prevent effective, efficient reforms from improving results in the public sector.

7. Major Findings and Conclusions

This chapter highlights the most important findings discussed in the foregoing chapters and offers broad conclusions based on the evidence as a whole.

Major Findings

Chapter 1 reviewed evidence on U.S. academic achievement and concluded that, despite having among the highest (and still rising) per student costs in the industrialized world, U.S. schools are among the poorest performers. At the high school level, the United States has among the worst academic achievement test scores of member countries of the Organization for Economic Cooperation and Development. The productivity (academic achievement per dollar spent) of public schools in the United States fell an estimated 55 to 73 percent between the 1970–71 and 1998–99 school years.

Since youngsters' future well-being and the nation's prosperity depend on educational effectiveness, the public, legislators, and parents are interested in the possibility that school choice may increase educational performance. To provide them with some guidance on that question, this book reviews a wide array of research on the effects of choice schools on their students and on students in neighboring traditional public schools.

Chapter 2 surveyed the research literature on the academic effects of charter schools. Because there are more than 4,000 charter schools in the United States enrolling more than one million students, they offer a sufficiently large database to conduct valid empirical research. Many charter schools are heavily regulated, subject to various obstacles, and less well funded than nearby traditional public schools. These handicaps prevent a fair test of market forces in education.

Despite these handicaps, charter schools perform well. The largest single-point-in-time study of charter schools involved nearly every charter school in the nation and its nearest neighboring traditional public school. The study showed that charter schools outperformed the comparison schools; that poor and Hispanic students achieved particularly well; and that outcomes improved as charter schools were given more autonomy, funding, and time to work out the initial startup kinks in their operations. Of 26 studies of achievement gains, 22 showed that charter schools yielded either a better or an equal effect. Three over-time studies and one random-assignment study found significant achievement gains by charter school students relative to traditional public school students. Five of seven studies examining the performance of individual charter school students over time showed positive achievement effects.

Charter schools are popular with parents who send their children to them as well as with the general public. Charter schools, on average, have succeeded despite the burdens of overregulation and while spending perhaps a fifth less than traditional public schools.

Chapter 3 reviewed research on public and private school voucher programs in the United States and elsewhere. Vouchers could be expected to improve student achievement and parental satisfaction because competition often brings out the best in people and organizations; because competitors provide benchmarks against which to measure all schools' performance; and because vouchers allow and encourage parents to more actively participate in their children's schooling, which in turn is positively related to student learning.

Eight random-assignment studies and three non-random-assignment studies of education vouchers all found positive effects on the academic achievement of some groups attending voucher schools but sometimes showed little or no effect on white students. No studies found a negative effect on achievement. The concentration of benefits on African-American students may be attributable to the larger numbers of black students in voucher programs, which makes the statistical detection of effects more likely.

The largest voucher program in the United States, Florida's McKay Scholarship Program, is for special needs children with a variety of educational disabilities including blindness and mental retardation. Though no analyses have been made of its possible achievement effects, it is much more highly regarded by parents than are traditional, nonchosen public schools.

Studies of voucher programs in Washington, DC, Cleveland, and Milwaukee show that they have reduced racial segregation by allowing students in segregated neighborhoods to cross public school boundaries to attend less-segregated schools of their choice. Surveys regularly show high levels of satisfaction among parents who participate in public and private voucher programs.

Public voucher programs in the United States exist only in a few large cities and generally are small in scope. Consequently, their success or failure does not constitute a good test of school vouchers. Programs in other countries are much larger and provide a better test of vouchers. The large majority of studies of these programs have found positive effects on student academic achievement.

Chapter 4 surveyed research on the effects of private schools. Since millions of parents voluntarily choose to enroll their children in them, private schools provide larger samples than charter and voucher schools. Offsetting this advantage, however, is the fact that random-assignment studies are nearly impossible, and controlling for socioeconomic status and other possible confounders is difficult and often controversial. In addition, grouping private schools, including independent and various kinds of parochial schools, together may hide important differences among them, and existing samples of private school subgroups may be too small to reveal statistically significant differences.

Most point-in-time studies show superior achievement of private schools, and all the well-designed studies in this field find positive effects after controlling for student socioeconomic status and other factors. Studies of achievement gains over time (value-added analyses) for students attending private schools tend to find a positive private school effect.

Catholic schools are the largest category of U.S. private schools, and their numbers allow the largest and longest-running studies. The most sophisticated achievement study showed superior Catholic school achievement, but a review of smaller studies showed mixed effects, with positive effects concentrated among African-American students. All studies, however, show that Catholic school graduation rates (with and without statistical regression controls) are higher than those of public schools.

Private schools appear to perform better, on average, than public schools at substantially less cost, even when the extra administrative and other costs borne by public schools are taken into account. Private schools are also more likely than public schools to have racial compositions resembling the population in their areas, and private school students are more likely to report greater levels of cross-racial friendship and fewer instances of racial fighting than public school students. Private schools also do better than public schools at fostering tolerance, civic participation, and social integration.

Chapter 5 examined research on the possible competitive effects on achievement in geopolitical regions such as states and metropolitan areas with differing degrees of school choice and local control of schools. Two literature reviews of some 140 studies showed that most studies show positive effects of increases in school choice opportunities on overall student achievement. The most rigorous 50-state study found strong positive effects. The largest international study of school choice effects, as indexed by the percentage of private schools in each of 39 countries, also showed strong positive effects on overall academic achievement. Constructive competition effects are also fostered among public schools in small and decentralized districts that rely more on local than on state funding and control.

Chapter 6 explained why public and parental satisfaction with schools is an important school outcome. Survey data show the general public's and parents' dissatisfaction with public schools and their considerable and growing support for school choice. Survey data also show that public educators have much lower standards and expectations than those of the public, parents, and students, which is a major reason why these consumers increasingly favor choice. These differences help explain why public school teachers' unions and administrators oppose proposals to introduce parental choice.

The U.S. Supreme Court ruled that parents may send their children to private, including parochial, schools and, more recently, that publicly funded vouchers for independent and parochial schools are constitutional. Since public authorities have severely restricted parents' right to choose public and private schools, satisfaction surveys loom large in determining the demand for charter schools and vouchers. The public and parents strongly support allowing parents to choose the schools their children attend. Parents whose children attend charter, voucher, and private schools tend to be more satisfied with those schools than parents whose children attend traditional public schools.

106

Conclusions

Based on these and other findings discussed in the foregoing chapters, Table 7-1 briefly summarizes the overall findings. There are 20 possible positive effects of four forms of choice on five educational outcomes. As suggested in the table, the possible effect findings can be classified as being supported by suggestive or conclusive evidence (none of the evidence for the possible findings was clearly inadequate).

The evidence supports every single one of the 20 possible choice effects, and the evidence is conclusive rather than suggestive for 14. It is statistically improbable that these overall results arose by chance. The results are about as consistent as can be found in the social sciences, and it thus seems clear that school choice works. Assuredly, choice schools do not compare favorably with traditional public schools in every single circumstance since, as was explained in the first chapter, the effects are based on average differences between choice and nonchoice schools. Moreover, it is impossible in science to prove the correctness of any hypothesis or theory. All conclusions are provisional until strong, contradictory evidence appears.

In addition to these caveats, several assumptions underlying Table 7-1 should be made explicit:

- Charter schools: The fast growth in the number of charter schools and the frequency with which they are oversubscribed are taken as one set of indications of parental satisfaction. The facts that charters are concentrated in cities often segregated by social class and ethnicity and that charter students cross traditional public school boundary lines are included as evidence of social integration.
- Vouchers: The conclusions about voucher effects on cost efficiency and parental satisfaction are based partly on extensive private school research. By definition, voucher-bearing students go to private schools, which fare well on these two criteria. In addition, of course, voucher programs are usually heavily oversubscribed; there are far more applicants than places for them.
- Though the effects of vouchers and charter schools are positive, on average, they may be underestimated for several reasons. The studies reviewed rarely take into account the fact that many

Table 7-1
Sufficiency of the Evidence for Positive School Choice Effects

Form of Choice	Point-in-Time Academic Achievement	Value-Added Over-Time Achievement Gains	Cost Efficiency	Parent Satisfaction, Citizens' Favorable Regard, or Both	Social Integration, Citizenship, or Both
Charter schools	Conclusive	Conclusive	Conclusive	Conclusive	Suggestive
Vouchers	Conclusive	Conclusive	Conclusive	Conclusive	Suggestive
Private schools	Conclusive	Suggestive	Conclusive	Conclusive	Conclusive
Competition	Conclusive	Suggestive	Suggestive	Conclusive	Suggestive

if not most of the voucher-bearing students are newly transferred to private schools, which, on average, are further from their homes, and the students need to adapt to new teachers, classmates, curricula, standards, and methods of teaching. Since many are new organizations, moreover, charter schools also have new students, and the schools themselves as organizations may take several years to hit their stride. In addition, charter schools and private schools, which voucher students attend, operate on fractions of the budgets of traditional public schools.

- The conclusions in the table complement and reinforce one another. Other things being equal, traditional public schools, on average, appear to perform less effectively and efficiently than either charter or private schools. This conclusion accords well with research on the performance of public and private organizations and on privatization of public services.

In short, given these overall findings and the consistency of the evidence, it may be confidently concluded that school choice generally works better than public school monopolies. Similarly, in the manufacturing and service industries that have been analyzed, nearly all reviews of studies show that markets provide higher quality, more customer choice, greater customer satisfaction, and lower costs than government provisioning. Studies of newly privatized government services also generally show such effects. The intensity of competition within geopolitical areas, moreover, allows, even requires, greater effectiveness and cost-efficiency on the part of surviving providers, public and private. The findings in this book are consistent with these widely documented conclusions, which have led to and are leading to increasing privatization in many countries including the United States.

Though sometimes greeted with initial pubic confusion and skepticism, charter schools and vouchers are becoming increasingly well supported as citizens gain knowledge of how they work, the results they produce, and their popularity with the families who use them. American parents, moreover, have rights to make the important decisions regarding their children's upbringing such as their names, where they live, and the people who treat them when they're ill.

In 1925 the U.S. Supreme Court upheld their right to choose a public or private school for their children, and in 2002 it upheld their right to do so with the help of a school choice program. As the research reviewed in this book shows, it would be good public policy to give all families ready access to that choice. It is ironic that Americans who regard themselves as free—perhaps as having the freest country in the world—have so little choice when it comes to their children's education. It is tragic that policy leaders, including governors, legislators, and school boards, have done so little to remedy that situation.

Notes

Chapter 1

1. Herbert J. Walberg, "Achievement in American Schools," in *A Primer on American Schools: An Assessment by the Koret Task Force on K–12 Education,* ed. Terry M. Moe (Stanford, CA: Stanford University, Hoover Institution Press, 2001), pp. 43–68. On costs, see Eric A. Hanushek, "Spending on Schools," in *A Primer on American Schools,* pp. 69–88.

2. Lynn Olson, "As AYP Bar Rises, More Schools Fail," *Education Week,* September 20, 2006, pp. 1, 20.

3. For a news account, see Diana Jean Schemo, "Grades Rise, but Reading Skills Do Not," *New York Times,* February 23, 2007, p. 3, http://www.nytimes.com/2007/02/22/education/22cnd-test.html?_r=1&hp&oref=slogin. For the full reports, see the National Assessment of Educational Progress, *Results of the 2005 School Transcript Study* and *Results of 2005 Grade 12 Mathematics and Reading Assessment,* http://nces.ed.gov/nationsreportcard/.

4. National Center for Public Policy and Higher Education, "The Need for State Leadership," *Cross Talk,* Summer 2005.

5. American College Test, *Reading between the Lines: What the ACT Reveals about College Readiness in Reading* (Iowa City, IA: ACT, 2006).

6. Education Trust, *College Results Online,* 2006, http://www2.edtrust.org/EdTrust/Press+Room/college+results.htm.

7. Christopher Clausen, "The New Ivory Tower," *Wilson Quarterly,* Autumn 2006, p. 32.

8. Public Agenda, "Are Parents and Students Ready for More Math and Science?" 2006, http://www.publicagenda.org/press/press_release_detail.cfm?list=67.

9. See Walberg; and Hanushek.

10. Caroline M. Hoxby, "School Choice and School Productivity, or Could School Choice Be a Tide That Lifts All Boats?" in *Economics of School Choice,* ed. Caroline Hoxby (Chicago: University of Chicago Press for the National Bureau of Economic Research, 2001).

11. See Walberg.

12. Eric A. Hanushek and Dennis D. Kimko, "Schooling, Labor-Force Quality, and the Growth of Nations," *American Economic Review* 90 (December 2000): 1184–1208.

13. Jill Casner-Lotto and Linda Barrington, *Are They Really Ready to Work? Employers' Perspectives on the Basic Knowledge and Applied Skills of New Entrants to the 21st Century Workforce,* Document 20154 (New York: Conference Board, 2006). See also http://www.heartland.org/Article.cfm?artId=20154.

14. "What Democrats May Do," *Wall Street Journal,* November 9, 2007, p. A2.

15. "The Battle for Brainpower: Survey of Talent," *The Economist,* October 7, 2006, pp. 1–24.

16. Ibid., p. 11.

17. David Wessel, "Why It Takes a Doctorate to Beat Inflation," *Wall Street Journal*, October 19, 2006, p. A2.

18. Herbert J. Walberg and Shio-Ling Tsai, "Matthew Effects in Education," *American Educational Research Journal* 20 (1984): 359–74.

19. Quoted in "Nations Anxious to See if They Can Make the Grade," *Financial Times*, October 18, 2006, p. 3.

20. "Asia and the World's Economy," *The Economist*, October 19, 2006.

21. Eric A. Hanushek. Eliott A. Jamison, and Dean T. Jamison, "The Effects of Educational Quality on Mortality Decline and Achievement Growth," *Economics of Education Review*, forthcoming.

22. David M. Cutler and Adriana Lleras-Muney, "Education and Health: Evaluating Theories and Evidence," unpublished paper, Harvard University, June 2006.

23. "The Battle for Brainpower," p. 11.

24. Ibid., p. 12.

25. Ibid., p. 14.

26. Ibid., p. 9.

27. U.S. Department of Labor, Bureau of Labor Statistics, "Charting the U.S. Labor Market in 2005," Chart 3-11, http://www.bls.gov/cps/labor2005/home.htm.

28. Quoted in ibid., pp. 23–24.

29. Andrew J. Coulson, *Market Education: The Unknown History* (New Brunswick, NJ: Transaction, 1999).

30. Charles L. Glenn, *Educational Freedom in Eastern Europe*, 2d ed. (Washington: Cato Institute, 1995); idem, *Choice of Schools in Six Nations* (Washington: U.S. Department of Education, 1988); and David Salisbury and James Tooley, eds., *What America Can Learn from School Choice in Other Countries* (Washington: Cato Institute, 2005).

31. Andrew J. Coulson, "The Cato Education Market Index," Cato Institute Policy Analysis no. 585, December 14, 2006.

32. Joseph L. Bast and Herbert J. Walberg, *Ten Principles of School Choice* (Chicago: Heartland Institute, 2006).

33. Anna Fifield, "Korea's Unlikely Internet Star," *Financial Times*, February 15, 2007, p. 9.

34. For an excellent summary of this nascent industry, see Steven F. Wilson, *Learning on the Job: When Business Takes on Public Schools* (Cambridge, MA: Harvard University Press, 2006).

Chapter 2

1. Gregg Vanourek, *State of the Charter School Movement 2005: Trends, Issues, and Indicators* (Washington: Charter School Leadership Council, 2005), p. 8, http://www.charterschoolleadershipcouncil.org/pdf/sotm2005.pdf.

2. Michael Petrilli, "Identity Crisis: Can Charter Schools Survive Accountability?" *Education Next*, Summer 2005, p. 57.

3. Robin J. Lake and Lydia Rainey, *Chasing the Blues Away: Charter Schools Scale Up in Chicago* (Washington: Progressive Policy Institute, 2005), p. 22.

4. Elizabeth Kneebone, Trinia Logue, Susan Cahn, and Michael McDunnah, *Here and Now: The Need for Performing Schools in Chicago's Neighborhoods* (Chicago: Illinois Facilities Fund, October, 2004), http://www.iff.org/resources/content/1/1/documents/cpsfullreport.pdf.

5. Lake and Rainey, p. 6.

6. George A. Clowes, "Polls Show Vouchers Are Popular and Would Be Widely Used," *School Reform News*, April 2004, http://www.heartland.org/Article.cfm?artId_15702.

7. Harwood Group, *Halfway Out the Door: Citizens Talk about Their Mandate for Public Schools* (Dayton, OH: Kettering Foundation, 1995), http://www.theharwoodgroup.com.

8. Caroline M. Hoxby, "Achievement in Charter Schools and Regular Public Schools in the United States: Understanding the Differences," December 2004, http://post.economics.harvard.edu/faculty/hoxby/papers.html.

9. Ibid., executive summary.

10. Ibid., p. 15.

11. Ibid., executive summary.

12. Caroline M. Hoxby, "If Families Matter Most," in *A Primer on America's Schools*, ed. Terry M. Moe (Stanford, CA: Hoover Institution Press, 2001), p. 113.

13. Herbert J. Walberg, "High Performance, High Poverty Schools, Districts, and States" in *Courting Failure*, ed. Eric Hanushek (Stanford, CA: Hoover Institution Press, in press).

14. Ibid., p. 13–14.

15. F. Howard Nelson, Bella Rosenberg, and Nancy Van Meter, "Charter School Achievement on the 2003 National Assessment of Educational Progress," American Federation of Teachers, 2005, www.aft.org.

16. National Center for Education Statistics, "The Nation's Report Card: America's Charter Schools: Results from the 2003 Pilot Study," 2005, www.nces.ed.gov.

17. Bryan C. Hassel, *Charter School Achievement: What We Know* (Chapel Hill, NC: Public Impact, July 2005), p. 2.

18. As emphasized in the introduction, studies of student achievement at a single point in time are likely to be weak for making causal inferences. Henry Braun, Frank Jenkins, and Wendy Grigg completed just such a study, which is entirely misleading. See Henry Braun, Frank Jenkins, and Wendy Grigg, "A Closer Look at Charter Schools Using Hierarchical Linear Modeling," NCES 2006–460, http://nces.ed.gov/nationsreportcard//pubs/studies/2006460.asp. As discussed further in Chapter 4, Paul E. Peterson and Elena Llaudet, "On the Public-Private School Achievement Debate," paper presented at the meetings of the American Political Science Association, Philadelphia, August 2006 provides detailed criticism of a similar public-private school comparison study with the same data and defective methodology. That study is "Comparing Private Schools and Public Schools Using Hierarchical Linear Models," NCES 2006-461, July 2006.

19. Jay P. Greene, Greg Forster, and Marcus A. Winters, "Apples to Apples: An Evaluation of Charter Schools Serving General Student Populations," Manhattan Institute Education Working Paper no. 1, July 2003.

20. Lewis C. Solmon and Pete Goldschmidt, "Comparison of Traditional Public Schools and Charter Schools on Retention, School Switching, and Achievement Growth," Goldwater Institute Policy Report no. 192, March 15, 2004.

21. Tom Loveless, Andrew P. Kelly, and Alice M. Henriques, "What Happens When Regular Public Schools Convert to Charter Schools?" Vanderbilt University, National Research and Development Center on School Choice, Competition, and Achievement, May 27, 2005.

22. Caroline M. Hoxby and Jonah E. Rockoff, "The Impact of Charter Schools on Student Achievement," November 2004, http://post.economics.harvard.edu/faculty/hoxby/papers.html. For a description of a new randomized experimental study being conducted by Mathematica, see http://www.mathematica-mpr.com/education/charterschools.asp.

23. Caroline M. Hoxby and Jonah E. Rockoff, "Findings from the City of Big Shoulders," *Education News* 4 (2005), http://www.hoover.org/publications/ednext/3217766.html.

24. Ibid.

25. Clive R. Belfield and Henry M. Levin, *Education Privatization: Causes, Consequences, and Planning Implications* (Paris: International Institute for Educational Planning, UNESCO, 2002), p. 56.

26. Vanourek, p. 24.

27. U.S. Government Accountability Office, "Charter Schools: To Enhance Education's Monitoring and Research, More Charter School Level Data Are Needed," January 2005, p. 28.

28. Caroline M. Hoxby, "How School Choice Affects the Achievement of Public School Students," in *Choice with Equity*, ed. Paul T. Hill (Stanford, CA: Hoover Institution Press, 2002), pp. 158, 162.

29. Ibid., p. 157.

30. Ibid., p. 161.

31. Kevin Booker, Scott Gilpatric, Timothy Gronberg, and Dennis Jansen, "The Effect of Charter Schools on Traditional Public School Students in Texas: Are Children Who Stay Behind Left Behind?" September 2005, http://zeus.econ.umd.edu/cgi-bin/conference/download.cgi?db_name = nawm2005&paper_id = 411.

32. Ibid., p. 20.

33. Ibid., p. 19.

34. George M. Holmes, Jeff Desimone, and Nicholas G. Rupp, "Friendly Competition: Does the Presence of Charters Spur Public Schools to Improve?" *Education Next*, Winter 2006, http://www.educationnext.org.

35. Ibid., p. 69.

36. Paul Teske, Mark Schneider, Jack Buckley, and Sara Clark, "Does Charter School Competition Improve Traditional Public Schools?" Manhattan Institute Center for Civic Innovation Civic Report no. 10, June 2000, p. 1.

37. Vanourek, p. 39.

38. Ibid., p. 38.

39. Ibid., p. 39.

40. Duncan McCully and Patricia J. Malin, "What Parents Think of New York's Charter Schools," Manhattan Institute Center for Civic Innovation Civic Report no. 37, June 2003.

41. Lewis C. Solmon, Kern Paark, and David Garcia, "Does Charter School Attendance Improve Test Scores? The Arizona Results," Goldwater Institute, 2003, p. 10. See also Lewis C. Solmon, "Findings from the 2002 Survey of Parents with Children in Arizona Charter Schools: How Parents Grade Their Charter Schools," Human Resources Policy Corporation, March 10, 2003.

42. Solomon, Paark, and Garcia, Table 6, p. 13.

43. "State Notes on Charter Schools from the Education Commission of the States," April 2003, cited in Theodore R. Sizer, "Don't Tie Us Down," *Education Next*, Summer 2005, p. 61.

44. Herbert J. Walberg, "Improving Educational Productivity: An Assessment of Extant Research," in *The Scientific Basis of Educational Productivity*, ed. Rena F. Subotnik and Herbert J. Walberg (Greenwich, CT: Information Age, 2006), pp. 103–60.

45. Vanourek, p. 30.

46. Chester E. Finn, Bryan C. Hassel, and Sheree Speakman, *Charter School Funding: Inequity's Next Frontier* (Washington: Thomas B. Fordham Foundation, 2005).

47. Cited in ibid., executive summary, p. viii.

Chapter 3

1. John C. Goodman and Matt Moore, "School Choice v. School Choice," National Center for Policy Analysis Policy Backgrounder no. 155, April 27, 2001, p. 6, http://www.ncpa.org/pub/bg/bg155/.

2. Paul E. Peterson, Jay P. Greene, William G. Howell, and William McCready, "Initial Findings from an Evaluation of School Choice Programs in Washington, D.C., and Dayton, Ohio," Harvard University Program on Education Policy and Governance Working Paper, 1998; and Paul E. Peterson, David Myers, and William G. Howell, "An Evaluation of the New York City School Choice Scholarships Program: The First Year," Harvard University Program on Education Policy and Governance Working Paper, 1998.

3. David Myers, Paul E. Peterson, David Mayer, Julia Chou, and William G. Howell, "School Choice in New York City after Two Years: An Evaluation of the School Choice Scholarships Program," Harvard University Program on Education Policy and Governance Working Paper, 2000, available from Mathematica Policy Research, http://www.mathematica-mpr.com/.

4. Daniel P. Mayer, Paul E. Peterson, David E. Myers, Christina Clark Tuttle, and William G. Howell, "School Choice in New York City after Three Years: An Evaluation of the School Choice Scholarships Program Final Report," Mathematica Policy Research Report no. 8404-045, February 19, 2002.

5. Jay P. Greene, "Vouchers in Charlotte," *Education Matters* 1, no. 2 (Summer 2001): 55–60.

6. Jay P. Greene, Paul E. Peterson, and Jiangtao Du, "School Choice in Milwaukee: A Randomized Experiment," in *Learning from School Choice*, ed. Paul E. Peterson and Bryan C. Hassel (Washington: Brookings Institution, 1998), pp. 335–56.

7. Cecilia Rouse, "Private School Vouchers and Student Achievement: An Evaluation of the Milwaukee Parental Choice Program," *Quarterly Journal of Economics* 113, no. 2 (May 1998): 593.

8. Kim K. Metcalf, "Evaluation of the Cleveland Scholarship and Tutoring Program, 1996–1999," Indiana University, 1999, p. 20.

9. Paul E. Peterson, William G. Howell, and Jay P. Greene, "An Evaluation of the Cleveland Voucher Program after Two Years," Harvard University Program on Education Policy and Governance, 1999. See also http://www.spa.ucla.edu/ps/pdf/S00/PS294/peterson-howell-greene(1999).pdf.

10. Jay P. Greene, "The Hidden Research Consensus for School Choice," in *Charters, Vouchers, and Public Education*, ed. Paul E. Peterson and David E. Campbell (Washington: Brookings Institution, 2001), p. 90.

11. Brian P. Gill, Michael Timpane, Karen E. Ross, and Dominic J. Brewer, "Rhetoric versus Reality: What We Know and What We Need to Know about Vouchers and Charter Schools," RAND Corporation, 2001; and Paul Teske and Mark Schneider, "What Research Can Tell Us about School Choice," *Journal of Policy Analysis and Management* 20 (Fall 2001): 609–31.

12. Paul E. Peterson, "Choice in American Education," in *A Primer on America's Schools*, ed. Terry M. Moe (Stanford, CA: Hoover Institution Press. 2001), pp. 274–75, http://hdc-www.harvard.edu/pepg/index.htm.

13. Gill, Timpane, Ross, and Brewer, pp. xiv–xv.

14. Dan Goldhaber, "The Interface between Public and Private Schooling," in *Improving Educational Productivity*, ed. David H. Monk, Herbert J. Walberg, and Margaret D. Wang (Greenwich, CT: Information Age Publishing, 2001), p. 64.

15. Patrick J. Wolf, "Looking Inside the Black Box: What School Factors Explain Voucher Gains in Washington, D.C.?" Georgetown University Public Policy Institute, 2005.

16. Ibid., p. 9.

17. Paul E. Peterson, "Thorough and Efficient Private and Public Schools," in *Courting Failure*, ed. Erik A. Hanushek (Stanford, CA: Stanford University Education Next Press, 2006), pp. 195–234.

18. Ibid., p. 217.

19. Caroline M. Hoxby, "How School Choice Affects the Achievement of Public School Students," in *Choice with Equity*, ed. Paul T. Hill (Stanford, CA: Hoover Institution Press, 2002), p. 150.

20. Carol Innerst, "Competing to Win: How Florida's A+ Plan Has Triggered Public School Reform," Center for Education Reform, April 2000, introduction, http://edreform.com/school_choice/compete.htm, cited in Goodman and Moore, p. 12.

21. Jay P. Greene, "An Evaluation of the Florida A+ Accountability and School Choice Program," Manhattan Institute Center for Civic Innovation, February 2001.

22. Jay P. Greene and Marcus A. Winters, "Competition Passes the Test," *Education Next* 4, no. 3 (2004): 7.

23. Martin R. West and Paul E. Peterson, *The Efficacy of Choice Threats within School Accountability Systems: Results from Legislatively Induced Experiments*, 2005, cited in Jay P. Greene and Marcus A. Winters, "An Evaluation of the Effect of D.C.'s Voucher Program on Public School Achievement and Racial Integration after One Year," Manhattan Institute Education Working Paper no. 10, January 2006, p. 4.

24. David N. Figlio and Cecilia E. Rouse, "Do Accountability and Voucher Threats Improve Low-Performing Schools?" NBER Working Paper no. W11597, September 2005, available at http://ssrn.com/abstract=800452.

25. Greene and Winters, "An Evaluation of the Effect of D.C.'s Voucher Program."

26. Jay P. Greene and Greg Forster, "Vouchers for Special Education Students: An Evaluation of Florida's McKay Scholarship Program," Manhattan Institute, 2003.

27. Christine Rossell, David J. Armor, and Herbert J. Walberg, eds., *School Desegregation in the 21st Century* (Westport, CT: Praeger, 2002).

28. Greene and Winters, "An Evaluation of the Effect of D.C.'s Voucher Program," p. 13.

29. *Digest of Education Statistics, 2002*, p. 73, Table 61, cited in Goodwin Liu and William L. Taylor, "School Choice to Achieve Desegregation," *Fordham Law Review* 74, no. 2 (2005): 791–824.

30. Jay P. Greene, "Choice and Community: The Racial, Economic, and Religious Context of Parental Choice in Cleveland," Buckeye Institute for Public Policy Solutions, November 1999.

31. Ibid.

32. Howard L. Fuller and Deborah Greiveldinger, "The Impact of School Choice on Racial Integration in Milwaukee Public Schools," American Education Reform Council, August 2002, p. 7.

33. Ibid., p. 3.

34. Ibid., p. 6.

35. Gregg Forster, "The Empirical Evidence on Vouchers and Segregation," *School Choice Issues*, September 2006, p. 19.

36. Government Accountability Office, "School Vouchers: Characteristics of Privately Funded Programs," Report to the Honorable Judd Gregg, U.S. Senate, GAO-02-752, September 2002, p. 19.

37. Ibid., p. 20.

38. Daniel P. Mayer, Paul E. Peterson, David E. Myers, Christina Clark Tuttle, and William G. Howell, "School Choice in New York City after Three Years: An Evaluation of the School Choice Scholarships Program," Mathematica Policy Research, February 2002, cited in Government Accountability Office, p. 21.

39. John F. Witte, *The Market Approach to Education: An Analysis of America's First Voucher Program* (Princeton, NJ: Princeton University Press, 2000), Table 4.3, p. 63.

40. Terry M. Moe, *Private Vouchers* (Stanford, CA: Hoover Institution Press, 1995).

41. F. Mikael Sandström and Fredrik Bergström, "School Vouchers in Practice: Competition Won't Hurt You!" *Journal of Public Economics* 89, nos. 2–3 (2005): 351–80. See also Fredrick Bergström and F. Mikael Sandström, *School Choice Works: The Case of Sweden* (Indianapolis, IN: Milton and Rose D. Friedman Foundation, 2003).

42. Andrew Coulson, "Market Education and Its Critics: Testing School Choice Criticisms against the International Evidence," in *What America Can Learn from School Choice in Other Countries*, ed. David Salisbury and James Tooley (Washington: Cato Institute, 2005), p. 152.

43. H. M. Patrinos, "Private Education Provision and Public Finance: The Netherlands as a Possible Model," National Center for the Study of Privatization in Education Occasional Paper no. 59, 2002; and G. Walford, "Funding for Private Schools in England and the Netherlands: Can the Piper Call the Tune?" National Center for the Study of Privatization in Education, 2000; both cited in Clive R. Belfield and Henry M. Levin, *Education Privatization: Causes, Consequences, and Planning Implications* (Paris: UNESCO/International Institute for Educational Planning, 2002), p. 57.

44. J. D. Levin, "Essays in the Economics of Education," Tinbergen Institute (Amsterdam) Research Series, 2002, cited in Belfield and Levin, p. 57.

45. Belfield and Levin, p. 58.

46. Ibid., p. 53; and Claudio Sapelli, "The Chilean Education Voucher System," in *What America Can Learn from School Choice in Other Countries*, p. 41.

47. Patrick J. McEwan, "The Effectiveness of Public, Catholic, and non-Religious Private Schools in Chile's Voucher System, *Education Economics* 9 (2001): 103–28, cited in Belfield and. Levin, pp. 53–54.

48. Sapelli, p. 58.

49. Ibid., p. 55.

50. Andrew J. Coulson, "How Markets Affect Quality," in *Educational Freedom in Urban America: Brown v. Board after Half a Century*, ed. David Salisbury and Casey Lartigue (Washington: Cato Institute, 2004), http://www.schoolchoices.org/roo/How_Markets_Affect_Quality.pdf. See also Francisco A Gallego, "Competencia y Resultados Educativos: Teoría y Evidencia para Chile," Central Bank of Chile Working Paper no. 150, April 2002.

51. Belfield and Levin, p. 54.

52. Ibid.

Chapter 4

1. See Herbert J. Walberg and Joseph L. Bast, *Capitalism and Education* (Stanford, CA: Hoover Institution Press, 2003), pp. 54–60.

2. James A. Johnson, Harold W. Collins, Victor L. Dupuis, and John H. Johansen, *Introduction to the Foundations of American Education*, 6th ed. (Boston: Allyn and Bacon, 1985).

3. John T. Wenders, "The Extent and Nature of Waste and Rent Dissatisfaction in U.S. Public Schools" *Cato Journal* 25 (2005): 222.

4. James S. Coleman, "Public Schools, Private Schools, and the Public Interest," *Public Interest* 64 (Summer 1981).

5. Martha Naomi Alt and Katherine Peter, "Private Schools: A Brief Portrait," in *The Condition of Education 2002* (Washington: U.S. Department of Education, 2002).

6. "Enrollments of Private High School Students in Elite Colleges and Universities," *Wall Street Journal*, September 15, 2006, p. W10.

7. Henry Braun, Frank Jenkins, and Wendy Grigg, "Comparing Private Schools and Public Schools Using Hierarchical Linear Models," U.S. Department of Education Institute of Education Sciences, National Center for Education Statistics, NCES 2006-461, 2006.

8. Paul E. Peterson and Elena Llaudet, "On the Public-Private School Achievement Debate," paper presented at the meetings of the American Political Science Association, Philadelphia, August 2006.

9. John E. Chubb and Terry Moe, *Politics, Markets, and America's Schools* (Washington: Brookings Institution, 1990).

10. Paul E. Peterson, "Thorough and Efficient Private and Public Schools" in *Courting Failure*, ed. Erik A. Hanushek (Stanford, CA: Stanford University Education Next Press, 2006), p. 221.

11. James Coleman and Thomas Hoffer, *Public and Private High Schools: The Impact of Communities* (New York: Basic Books, 1987).

12. Anthony Bryk, Valerie Lee, and Paul Holland, *Catholic Schools and the Common Good* (Cambridge, MA: Harvard University Press, 1993).

13. Derek Neal, "The Effects of Catholic Secondary Schooling on Educational Achievement," *Journal of Labor Economics* 15, no. 1 (1997): 100.

14. Patrick J. McEwan, "Comparing the Effectiveness of Public and Private Schools," Teachers College, Columbia University, National Center for the Study of Privatization in Education, Occasional Paper no. 3, 2000.

15. Eric R. Eide, Dan D. Goldhaber, and Mark H. Showalter, "Does Catholic High School Attendance Lead to Attendance at a More Selective College?" *Social Science Quarterly* 85, no. 5 (2005): 1335–52.

16. Thomas Sowell, "Patterns of Black Excellence," *Public Interest*, Spring 1976, pp. 26–58.

17. Thomas Sowell, "Black Excellence: The Case of Dunbar High School," *Public Interest* 35 (Spring 1974): 1–21.

18. Chubb and Moe, p. 182.

19. Valerie Lee, "Catholic Lessons for Public Schools," in *New Schools for a New Century*, ed. Diane Ravitch (New Haven, CT: Yale University Press, 1997), pp. 147–63.

20. Paul E. Peterson and Herbert J. Walberg, "Urban Catholic Schools Excel Academically, Struggle Financially," *School Reform News* (Heartland Institute), April 2005, http://www.heartland.org/Article.cfm?artId = 16672. For additional details, see William Howell and Paul E. Peterson, *The Education Gap: Vouchers and Urban Schools* (Washington: Brookings Institution, 2002).

21. Peterson and Walberg.

22. Charles C. Wolf, *Markets or Governments: Choosing between Imperfect Alternatives* (Cambridge, MA: MIT Press, 1988); and E. S. Savas, *Privatization and Public-Private Partnerships* (New York: Chatham House, 2000).

23. John Hilke, *Cost Savings from Privatization: A Compilation of Study Findings* (Los Angeles: Reason Foundation, 1993).

24. Andrew J. Coulson, "Arizona Public and Private Schools: A Statistical Analysis," Goldwater Institute, 2006, http://www.goldwaterinstitute.org/Common/Files/Multimedia/1137.pdf.

25. Wenders.

26. David F. Salisbury, "What Does a Voucher Buy? A Closer Look at the Cost of Private Schools," Cato Institute Policy Analysis no. 486, August 28, 2003, http://www.cato.org/pubs/pas/pa486.pdf; and National Center for Education Statistics, *Digest of Education Statistics, 2002,* Table 61, http://nces.ed.gov/pubs2003/2003060b.pdf.

27. David Salisbury, "Saving Money and Improving Education: How School Choice Can Help States Reduce Expenditure Costs," Cato Institute Policy Analysis no. 551, October 4, 2005.

28. An issue that clouds such cost comparisons is the possible differences in percentages of special needs and poor students in the public and private schools since public schools are normally eligible for (and receive) extra funds for each such student. A more fundamental issue is the classification of special needs students. With the exceptions of fully or partially blind and deaf students, classifications of students in need of special programs are highly unreliable, that is, experts lack agreement on which classification schemes to use and on which students to place in such categories as normal, learning disabled, mildly mentally handicapped, and behaviorally disordered. Special educators may be motivated to classify increasing percentages of students as in need of their services, which brings increased funding and administrative and teaching jobs to public school systems. Further complicating policy is the finding that, on average, special needs students who are "mainstreamed," that is, placed in regular classes, do better than those who are segregated into special programs, They may do better since they are not stigmatized and they, their classmates, and their teachers have higher expectations for their performance. For these reasons, private schools that avoid questionable psychological categorization of students are both more effective and less costly. For findings about and analyses of these issues, see Margaret C. Wang, Maynard C. Reynolds, and Herbert J. Walberg, eds., *Handbook of Special Education,* 4 vols. (London: Pergamon, 1987–89); and Chester E. Finn Jr., Andrew J. Rotherham, and Charles R. Hokanson Jr., eds., *Rethinking Special Education for a New Century* (Washington: Progressive Policy Institute, 2001).

29. Salisbury, "Saving Money and Improving Education," p. 9.

30. Ibid., p. 10.

31. Ibid., p. 12.

32. David Campbell, "Making Democratic Education Work: Schools, Social Capital and Civic Education," paper presented at the Conference on Charter Schools, Vouchers, and Public Education, Harvard University, March 9–10, 2000.

33. Daniel A. McFarland and Carlos Starmanns. "Student Government and Political Socialization," unpublished manuscript, Stanford University, http://www.stanfordalumni.org/news/magazine/2004/sepoct/features/politics.htm.

34. Patrick J. Wolf, Jay P. Greene, Brett Kleitz, and Kristina Thalhammar, "Private Schooling and Political Tolerance: Evidence from College Students in Texas," paper presented at the Conference on Vouchers, Charters, and Public Education, Harvard University, March 2000, p. 20.

35. David E. Campbell, "Vote Often: Creating Civic Norms," *Education Next*, Summer 2005, p. 69.

36. Jay P. Greene, Joseph Giammo, and Nicole Mellow, "The Effect of Private Education on Political Participation, Social Capital and Tolerance: An Examination of the Latino National Political Survey," *Georgetown Public Policy Review* 5, no. 1 (Fall 1999), summarized in Jay P. Greene, "A Survey of Results from Voucher Experiments: Where We Are and What We Know," Manhattan Institute Civic Report no. 11, July 2000, p. 11, http://www.manhattan-institute.org/html/cr_11.htm.

37. One study suggests that, under a completely free choice system, schools would tend to be segregated—not by social class or race but by ability as in the case of American colleges and universities. See Dennis Epple, "Competition between Private and Public Schools, Vouchers, and Peer Group Effects," *American Economic Review* 88 (March 1998): 33–62.

38. Helen Ladd and Edward Fiske, *School Choice in New Zealand: A Cautionary Tale* (Washington: Brookings Institution, 2000); Amy Stuart Wells, "Sociology of School Choice: Why Some Win and Others Lose in the Educational Marketplace," in *School Choice: Examining the Evidence*, ed. Edith Rasell and R. Rothstein (Washington: Economic Policy Institute, 1993); and J. Douglas Williams and Frank H. Echols, "The Scottish Experience of Parental School Choice," in *School Choice*; all cited in Greene, "A Survey of Results from Voucher Experiments."

39. Jay P. Greene, "Civic Values in Public and Private Schools," in *Learning from School Choice*, ed. Paul E. Peterson and Bryan C. Hassel (Washington: Brookings Institution, 1998), pp. 83–106, cited in Greene, "A Survey of Results from Voucher Experiments," p. 9.

40. Jay P. Greene, "Civic Values in Public and Private Schools," cited in Greene, "A Survey of Results from Voucher Experiments," p. 12.

41. Greene, "Civic Values in Public and Private Schools," cited in Greene, "A Survey of Results from Voucher Experiments," p. 9.

42. Jay P. Greene, "The Racial, Economic, and Religious Context of Parental Choice in Cleveland," paper presented at the Association for Public Policy Analysis and Management meeting, Washington, November 1999, http://www.ksg.harvard.edu/pepg/papers.htm, cited in Greene, "A Survey of Results from Voucher Experiments," p. 10.

43. Andrew J. Coulson, "How Markets Affect Quality: Testing a Theory of Market Education against the International Evidence," in *Educational Freedom and Urban America*, ed. David Salisbury and Casey Lartigue Jr. (Washington: Cato Institute, 2004).

44. James Tooley and Pauline Dixon, *Private Education Is Good for the Poor: A Study of Private Schools Serving the Poor in Low-Income Countries* (Washington: Cato Institute, 2006), pp. 2–3.

45. Priyanka Anand, Alejandra Mizala, and Andea Repetto, *Using Scholarships to Estimate the Effect of Government Subsidized Private Education on Academic Achievement in Chile* (Washington: American Institutes for Research, 2006).

Chapter 5

1. Paul Teske and Mark Schneider, "What Research Can Tell Policymakers about School Choice," *Journal of Policy Analysis and Management* 20 (Fall 2001): 609–31.

2. Ibid., p. 609.

3. Ibid., abstract.

4. Ibid., p. 619.

5. Clive R. Belfield and Henry M. Levin, *The Effects of Competition on Educational Outcomes: A Review of U.S. Evidence* (New York: National Center for the Study of Privatization in Education, Teachers College, Columbia University, September 2001), p. 1, http://www.ncspe.org/keepout/papers/00035/585_OP35.pdf.

6. Ibid., Table 1, "Summary of the Effects of Increases in Competition by One Standard Deviation," p. 47.

7. Ludger Woessman, "Why Students in Some Countries Do Better," *Education Next*, no. 2 (2001): 5, http://www.educationnext.org/20012/67.html.

8. Ibid., p. 2.

9. Ibid., p. 11.

10. Jay P. Greene, "Education Freedom Index," Manhattan Institute Civic Report no. 14, September 2000, http://www.manhattan-institute.org/html/cr_14.htm.

11. Ibid.

12. Andrew J. Coulson, "The Cato Education Market Index" Cato Institute Policy Analysis no. 585, December 13, 2006, p. 20.

13. Charles Tiebout, "A Pure Theory of Local Public Expenditures," *Journal of Political Economy* 64 (1956): 416–24.

14. For a recent review of Tiebout competition among jurisdictions and schools, see William Fischel, "The Courts and Public School Finance: Judge-Made Centralization and Economic Research" in *Handbook on the Economics of Education*, ed. Eric Hanushek and Finis Welch (London: Elsevier, forthcoming).

15. Herbert J. Walberg and Herbert J. Walberg III, "Losing Local Control," *Educational Researcher*, June–July 1993, pp.19–26. See also Herbert J. Walberg, "Losing Local Control of Education: Cost and Quality Implications," Heartland Institute Policy Brief no. 59, November 22, 1993, http:// www.heartland.org/pdf//21764i.pdf.

16. Melvin V. Borland and Roy M. Howsen, "On the Determination of the Critical Level of Market Concentration in Education," *Economics of Education Review* 12, no. 2 (1993): abstract.

17. Albert O. Hirschman used this index earlier, and subsequently it is termed the Herfindahl-Hirschman Index.

18. Lisa Barrow and Cecilia Elena Rouse, "Using Market Valuation to Assess the Importance and Efficiency of Public School Spending," paper presented at Annual Meeting of the American Educational Finance Association, in Econometric Society, Econometric Society World Congress 2000 Contributed Papers series, no. 1446, 2000, http://ideas.repec.org/s/ecm/wc2000.html.

19. Clive R. Belfield and Henry M. Levin, *The Effects of Competition on Educational Outcomes: A Review of U.S. Evidence* (New York: National Center for the Study of Privatization in Education, Teachers College, Columbia University, March 2002).

20. Caroline M. Hoxby, "How School Choice Affects the Achievement of Public School Students," in *Choice with Equity*, ed. Paul T. Hill (Stanford, CA: Hoover Institution Press, 2002), pp. 141–78.

21. Ibid., Table 8, "Effect of Traditional Inter-District Choice on Public School Students' Achievement," p. 173.

22. Jay P. Greene and Marcus A. Winters, "The Effect of Residential School Choice on Public High School Graduation Rates," Manhattan Institute Education Working Paper no. 9, April 2005.

23. David Tyack, *The One Best System: A History of American Urban Education* (Cambridge, MA: Harvard University Press, 1974); and David Tyack and Larry Cuban, *Tinkering toward Utopia: A Century of Public School Reform* (Cambridge, MA: Harvard University Press, 1995).

24. National Center for Education Statistics, *Digest of Education Statistics Tables and Figures 2003*, Table 85, "Number of Public School Districts and Public and Private Elementary Schools: Selected Years, 1869–70 to 2001–02," http://nces.ed.gov/ programs/digest/d03/tables/dt085.asp.

25. Greene and Winters, conclusion.

26. Montana ranks about exactly average in education spending per student, adjusted for regional cost differences (2002) at $7,772 per pupil compared with the $7,734 U.S. average. "Quality Counts 2005: No Small Change—Targeting Money toward Student Performance," *Education Week* 24, no. 17 (January 8, 2005): 102.

27. See student achievement rankings in National Assessment of Educational Progress, *The Nation's Report Card* (Washington: National Center for Education Statistics, 2006); and state profile for Montana at http://nces.ed.gov/nationsreportcard/ states/profile.asp.

28. National Center for Education Statistics, Table 93, "Public Elementary and Secondary Schools and Enrollment, by Type and Size of School: 2001–02," http:// nces.ed.gov/programs/digest/d03/tables/dt093.asp. The average number of students per school in 2001–02 was 520. Other statistics come from David Strang, "The Administrative Transformation of American Education: School District Consolidation, 1938–1980," *Administrative Science Quarterly* (1987): 352–66, cited in Walberg and Walberg.

29. Walberg and Walberg, pp. 19–26.

30. Ibid., p. 5.

31. Terry M. Moe, "A Union by Any Other Name," *Education Next*, Fall 2001, http://www.educationnext.org/20013/38moe.html.

32. Belfield and Levin.

33. National Center for Education Statistics, Table 86, "Number of Public School Districts and Enrollment, by Size of District: Selected Years, 1989–90 to 2001–02," http://nces.ed.gov/programs/digest/d03/tables/dt086.asp.

34. Elaine Allensworth, "Graduation and Dropout Trends in Chicago: A Look at Cohorts of Students from 1991 to 2004," Chicago Consortium for School Research, 2005, http://ccsr.uchicago.edu/content/publications.php?pub_id = 61&list = t.

35. National Assessment of Educational Progress, *The Nation's Report Card.*

36. William D. Eggers, Lisa Snell, Robert Wavra, and Adrian T. Moore, "Driving More Money into the Classroom: The Promise of Shared Services," Reason Foundation and Deloitte Research LLC, October 2005, http://www.reason.org/ps339.pdf.

37. Ibid.

38. See John Yinger, Howard S. Bloom, Axel Borch-Supan, and Helen F. Ladd, *Property Taxes and Housing Values* (Boston, MA: Academic Press, 1988).

39. Caroline Minter Hoxby, "Local Property Tax–Based Funding of Public Schools," Heartland Institute, May 19, 1997, pp. 1–2. See also idem, "Does Competition among Public Schools Benefit Students and Taxpayers? Evidence from Natural Variation in School Districting," National Bureau of Economic Research Working Paper no. 4979, 1994; and Melvin Borland and Roy Howsen, "Student Academic Achievement and the Degree of Market Concentration in Education," *Economics of Education Review* 389 (1992): 31–39.

Chapter 6

1. James W. Skillen, ed., *The School Choice Controversy: What Is Constitutional?* (Grand Rapids, MI: Baker Book House, 1993); and Virgil C. Blum, *Freedom of Choice in Education* (New York: Macmillan, 1958).

2. Steven Arons, *Short Route to Chaos* (Amherst: University of Massachusetts Press, 1997); R. McCarthy, D. Oppewal, W. Peterson, and G. Spykman, *Society, State and Schools: A Case for Structural and Confessional Pluralism* (Grand Rapids, MI: William B. Eerdmans, 1981); and D. D. McGarry and L. Ward, eds., *Educational Freedom and the Case for Government Aid to Students in Independent Schools* (Milwaukee, WI: Bruce, 1966).

3. U.S. Supreme Court, *Pierce v. Society of Sisters* (1925) at 12.

4. U.S. Supreme Court, *Zelman v. Simmons-Harris* (2002) at 32.

5. For a complete defense of this statement, see Joseph L. Bast and Herbert J. Walberg, "Can Parents Choose the Best Schools for Their Children?" *Economics of Education Review* 23 (2004): 431–40.

6. John E. Coons and S. D. Sugarman, *Education by Choice: The Case for Family Control* (Troy, NY: Educator's International Press, 1978), p. 47.

7. Ibid., p. 51.

8. Andrew J. Coulson, *Market Education: The Unknown History* (New Brunswick, NJ: Transaction, 1999), p. 260. See http://www.cato.org/people/coulson.html for additional Coulson references and information.

9. U.S. Department of Education, "National Household Survey, 1993," cited in Coulson, *Market Education*.

10. Caroline M. Hoxby, "If Families Matter Most," in *A Primer on America's Schools*, ed. Terry M. Moe (Stanford, CA: Hoover Institution Press, 2001), p. 117.

11. Milton Friedman and Rose Friedman, *Free to Choose* (New York: Harcourt Brace Jovanovich, 1980), p. 160.

12. George A. Clowes, "Polls Show Vouchers Are Popular and Would Be Widely Used," *School Reform News*, April 2004.

13. Public Agenda, "On Thin Ice: How Advocates and Opponents Could Misread the Public's View on Vouchers and Charter Schools," 1999.

14. Harwood Group, "Halfway Out the Door: Citizens Talk about Their Mandate for Public Schools," Kettering Foundation, 1995, http://www.theharwoodgroup.com.

15. Lowell C. Rose and Alec M. Gallup, "The 38th Annual Phi Delta Kappa/Gallup Poll of the Public's Attitudes toward the Public Schools," Phi Delta Kappa International, 2006.

16. Terry Moe, "Cooking the Questions," *Education Next*, 2002, pp. 70–72, http://www.educationnext.org/20021/70.html.

17. "New Evidence Calls PDK School Choice Poll into Question," Milton and Rose Friedman Foundation, news release, August 23, 2005, http://www.friedmanfoundation.org/news/2005-08-23.html.

18. Education Testing Service, "Ready for the Real World? Americans Speak on High School Reform," public opinion research conducted by Peter D. Hart and David Winston, June 2005, http://ftp.ets.org/pub/corp/2005execsum.pdf.

19. Peter D. Hart Research Associates and Public Opinion Strategies, "Rising to the Challenge: Are High School Graduates Ready for College and Work? Key Findings from Surveys among Public High School Graduates, College Instructors, and Employers," February 2005 (survey conducted December 2004–January 2005 for Achieve, Inc.).

20. Rose and Gallup.

21. E. D. Tab, "Parent and Family Involvement in Education: 2002–2003," National Center for Education Statistics, National Household Education Survey, 2005, Table 13, p. 45.

22. Terry Moe, *Schools, Vouchers, and the American Public* (Washington: Brookings Institution, 2001), p. 69.

23. Glover Park Group. "Poll Finds Broad Support for Public Charter Schools," 2006.

24. U.S. Department of Education National Center for Education Statistics, "1.1 Million Homeschooled Students in the United States in 2003," 2004, http://nces.ed.gov/nhes/homeschool/.

25. Isabel Lyman, "Home Schooling: Back to the Future," Cato Institute Policy Analysis no. 294, January 7, 1998.

26. Luis Huerta, Maria-Fernanda González, and Chad d'Entremont, "Cyber and Home School Charter Schools: Defining New Forms of Public Schooling, *Peabody Journal of Education* 81, no. 1 (2006): 103–39.

27. Mark Schneider and Jack Buckley, "Can Modern Technologies Cross the Digital Divide to Enhance Choice and Build Stronger Communities?" Columbia University Teachers College National Center for the Study of Privatization in Education Occasional Paper no. 7, October 2000.

28. Amos Bradley, "Survey Reveals Teens Yearn for High Standards," *Education Week*, February 12, 1997, p. 12.

29. James Johnson and Samuel Farkas, "Getting By: What American Teenagers Really Think about Their Schools," Public Agenda, 1997.

30. Jeff Archer, "District Leaders Said Not to Share Urgency for Education Reform," *Education Week*, October 4, 2006, p. 7.

31. Harris Interactive, "The MetLife Survey of the American Teacher 2001," 2001.

32. Theodore Sizer, *Horace's Compromise: The Dilemma of the American High Schools* (Boston: Houghton Mifflin, 1984).

33. Tom Loveless, *The 2006 Brown Center Report on American Education* (Washington: Brookings Institution, 2006), http://www.brookings.edu/press/books/2006browncenterreportonamericaneducation.htm.

34. S. Farkas and J. Johnson, "Different Drummers: How Teachers of Teachers View Public Education," Public Agenda, 1997.

35. On the basis of data for the 2003–2004 school year from 29 states reporting from September 1, 2004, 13 percent of schools nationwide have "needs improvement" status and 30.4 percent failed to make AYP. Calculated from data in Lynn Olson, "Data Shows Schools Making Progress on Federal Goals," *Education Week* 24, no. 2 (September 8, 2004): 1, 24–28; and in John E. Chubb, ed., *Within Our Reach: How America Can Educate Every Child* (Lanham, MD: Rowman and Littlefield, 2005), p. 1.

36. William Howell, "Switching Schools? A Closer Look at Parents' Initial Interest in and Knowledge about Choice Provisions of No Child Left Behind," *Peabody Journal of Education* 81, no. 1 (2006): 140–79.

37. Paul E. Peterson, "A Conflict of Interest: District Regulation of School Choice and Supplemental Services," in *Within Our Reach*, pp. 152–53.

38. Ibid., p. 152.

Index

public–private cost comparisons, 1,
68–72, 71t, 105
religious. *See* religious and parochial
schools
social integration, 74–75, 105–6, 107,
108t
summary and conclusions, 61, 76–77,
105–6, 107–10, 108t
tolerance and, 71–73, 75, 106
transfers to, 42, 43t, 48
weighted tuition estimate, 70
privatization of education, Czech
Republic, 53
productivity of schools, 3–4, 15, 103
Progress Analytics Institute and Public
Impact, 32
Progressive Policy Institute, charter
school study, 19–20
Public Agenda survey, 94, 98, 99–100
public opinion/views, 8
charter schools, 29–31, 96–97
polls, 93–101, 106
public policy, 8
public/private hybrid institutions, 15
public schools. *See* traditional public
school systems
Public Trust survey, 98–99
"A Pure Theory of Local
Expenditures," 83

quasi-experiments with statistical
adjustments, about, 10

racial-ethnic groups
benchmark statistics, 2
integration, private schools, 74–75,
105–6
integration, vouchers, 47–49
See also specific groups
RAND Corporation, 41
randomized field trials/random-
assignment study, 12, 83–84
about, 10, 77
charter schools, 25–26
voucher programs, 38–39, 104
reforms, 8
regression analyses. *See* correlational
(regression) analyses
regulations
charter schools, 31–32, 33, 103–4
private school, 52, 68–69
public school, 16
religious and parochial schools
achievement, 66–67, 105–6

Catholic schools, 62, 66–67, 68–69,
73, 105
costs per student, 68
parental satisfaction, 96
vouchers, 48, 49, 52, 53, 106
Repetto, Andrea, 76
research caveats and assumptions, 13,
107, 109
research considerations, 9–13
flaws, 12, 13, 65
reviews of research. *See* literature
reviews
Rockoff, Jonah, 25–26
Rouse, Cecilia, 39, 45
Rupp, Nicholas G., 29

safety issues and concerns, 3, 30, 47, 54
Salisbury, David, 71–72
San Antonio HORIZON program
(Texas), 36, 50
sanctions, 2
Sapelli, Claudio, 53–54
Schleicher, Andreas, 6
Schneider, Mark, 29, 80
Scholarship and Tutoring Program
(Ohio), 39–41, 49
scholarship studies, 38–41, 49, 50
*See also specific cities, states, and
programs by name*
school autonomy, 65, 67–69, 104
school choice, 7–8, 101, 103, 106
aptitude and achievement associated
with, 82
comprehensive literature reviews
summary, 79–80, 106
costs, 8, 9, 71–72, 97–98. *See also* per
pupil costs and spending
geopolitical effects. *See* geopolitical
area effects
positive effects, findings, 107–10, 108t
taxonomy, 13–16
See also specific choices, e.g., charter
schools, vouchers, *etc.*
school districts, size and competition
considerations, 15, 83–85
school performance, standardized
achievement tests and, 9
school spending, 2
ratio of achievement to, 3
schools in need of improvement, 2
segregation, vouchers and, 35, 37, 54,
104–5
Showalter, Mark H., 67
single-point-in-time studies

130

About the Author

Herbert J. Walberg is a distinguished visiting fellow at Stanford University's Hoover Institution and a project investigator at the Vanderbilt University Center of School Choice, Competition, and Achievement. Awarded a Ph.D. by the University of Chicago, he taught at Harvard University and the University of Illinois at Chicago for 35 years. He has written and edited more than 55 books and has written roughly 350 articles on such topics as educational achievement, research methods, and exceptional human accomplishments. Among his latest books are the *International Encyclopedia of Educational Evaluation, Education and Capitalism,* and *Psychology and Educational Practice.*

A fellow of five academic organizations including the American Association for the Advancement of Science, the American Psychological Association, and the Royal Statistical Society, Walberg is also a founding fellow of the International Academy of Education, headquartered in Brussels. He edits for the academy a booklet series on effective educational practices, which is distributed to education leaders in more than 120 countries and on the Internet. He is a trustee of the Foundation for Teaching Economics and chairs the boards of the Heartland Institute and the Beck Foundation.

Walberg has given invited lectures to educators and policymakers in Australia, Belgium, China, England, France, Germany, Italy, Israel, Japan, the Netherlands, South Africa, Sweden, Taiwan, Venezuela, and the United States. He has frequently testified before U.S. congressional committees, state legislators, and federal courts. He was a founding member and chaired the Design and Analysis Committee of the National Assessment Governing Board, the body that sets policy for the National Assessment of Educational Progress, which is given the mission to measure the K–12 school achievement trends in the major school subjects. He currently serves on the presidentially appointed, Senate approved National Board for Education Sciences.

Cato Institute

Founded in 1977, the Cato Institute is a public policy research foundation dedicated to broadening the parameters of policy debate to allow consideration of more options that are consistent with the traditional American principles of limited government, individual liberty, and peace. To that end, the Institute strives to achieve greater involvement of the intelligent, concerned lay public in questions of policy and the proper role of government.

The Institute is named for *Cato's Letters*, libertarian pamphlets that were widely read in the American Colonies in the early 18th century and played a major role in laying the philosophical foundation for the American Revolution.

Despite the achievement of the nation's Founders, today virtually no aspect of life is free from government encroachment. A pervasive intolerance for individual rights is shown by government's arbitrary intrusions into private economic transactions and its disregard for civil liberties.

To counter that trend, the Cato Institute undertakes an extensive publications program that addresses the complete spectrum of policy issues. Books, monographs, and shorter studies are commissioned to examine the federal budget, Social Security, regulation, military spending, international trade, and myriad other issues. Major policy conferences are held throughout the year, from which papers are published thrice yearly in the *Cato Journal*. The Institute also publishes the quarterly magazine *Regulation*.

In order to maintain its independence, the Cato Institute accepts no government funding. Contributions are received from foundations, corporations, and individuals, and other revenue is generated from the sale of publications. The Institute is a nonprofit, tax-exempt, educational foundation under Section 501(c)3 of the Internal Revenue Code.

CATO INSTITUTE
1000 Massachusetts Ave., N.W.
Washington, D.C. 20001
www.cato.org